# HISTORY OF CANON LAW

Louvain Theological and Pastoral Monographs is a publishing venture whose purpose is to provide those involved in pastoral ministry throughout the world with studies inspired by Louvain's long tradition of theological excellence within the Roman Catholic Tradition. The volumes selected for publication in the series are expected to express some of today's finest reflection on current theology and pastoral practice.

**Members of the Editorial Board**

**The Executive Committee:**

Raymond F. Collins, Catholic University of Leuven, chairman
Thomas P. Ivory, The American College, Catholic University of Leuven
Joël Delobel, Catholic University of Leuven
Lambert Leijssen, Catholic University of Leuven
Terrence Merrigan, Catholic University of Leuven, secretary

**Members at Large:**

Raymond E. Brown, Union Theological Seminary, New York
Juliana Casey, The Catholic Health Association of the United States
José M. de Mesa, East Asian Pastoral Institute, Manila, Philippines
Catherine Dooley, The Catholic University of America
Mary Grey, The Catholic University of Nijmegen, the Netherlands
James J. Kelly, Trinity College, Dublin, Ireland
Maria Goretti Lau, Holy Spirit Study Centre, Hong Kong
Donatus Mathenge, Nyeri Catholic Secretariat, Nyeri, Kenya
Michael Putney, Pius XII Provincial Seminary, Banyo, Australia
Ronald Rolheiser, Newman Theological College, Edmonton, Alberta, Canada
Donald P. Senior, Catholic Theological Union, Chicago
James J. Walter, Loyola University of Chicago

LOUVAIN THEOLOGICAL & PASTORAL MONOGRAPHS
— 5 —

# HISTORY OF CANON LAW

## CONSTANT VAN DE WIEL

PEETERS PRESS
LOUVAIN

ISBN 90-6831-212-X
D. 1991/0602/40

# TABLE OF CONTENTS

Preface . . . . . . . . . . . . . . . . . 9

Introduction: Concepts and Terms, Sources, and Legal Discipline . . . . . . . . . . . . . . . . 11

First Period
## FROM THE FOUNDATION OF THE CHURCH TO GREGORY VII (1073-1085)

Chapter I
Historical Framework . . . . . . . . . . . . 29

   A) The Church in the Eastern Roman Empire . . . 30
   B) The Church in the Western Roman Empire . . . 32

Chapter II
Documentary Sources . . . . . . . . . . . . 36

First Centuries . . . . . . . . . . . . . . 36

From 313 up until ca. 850 . . . . . . . . . . 40

   A) In the East . . . . . . . . . . . . . . 41
      Chronological Collections . . . . . . . . . 41
      Systematic Collections . . . . . . . . . . 42
   B) In the West . . . . . . . . . . . . . . 45
      Chronological Collections . . . . . . . . . 45
      Systematic Collections . . . . . . . . . . 52
   C) Other Collections . . . . . . . . . . . . 55
      Collections of Civil Law . . . . . . . . . 55
      *Libri paenitentiales* . . . . . . . . . . . 59
      Liturgical Books . . . . . . . . . . . . 62
      Collections of formulas . . . . . . . . . . 63
      *Capitula episcoporum* or *Statuta dioecesana* . . . 64
      Collections of "False" Documents . . . . . . 65

From the ninth century to Gregory VII . . . . . . 68

Chapter III
The Science of Law . . . . . . . . . . . . . 72

Second Period
FROM THE GREGORIAN REFORM TO THE COUNCIL OF TRENT
(Second half of the eleventh century to 1545)

Chapter I
Historical Context . . . . . . . . . . . . . 75

- A) Centralization of Papal Power . . . . . . . 75
- B) New Ways to Perfection . . . . . . . . . 80
- C) The Universities . . . . . . . . . . . . 91

Chapter II
Documentary Sources . . . . . . . . . . . 94

- A) Gregorian Collections . . . . . . . . . . 94
- B) The *Decretum Gratiani* . . . . . . . . . . 98
- C) The *Quinque Compilationes Antiquae* . . . . . 102
- D) The Decretals of Gregory IX . . . . . . . . 105
- E) *Liber Sextus Bonifatii VIII* . . . . . . . . 108
- F) *Constitutiones Clementinae* . . . . . . . . 109
- G) The *Extravangantes* . . . . . . . . . . . 110
- H) Other Collections . . . . . . . . . . . . 111

Chapter III
The Science of Law and its Practitioners . . . . . 115

- A) The Decretists . . . . . . . . . . . . . 115
- B) The First Decretalists . . . . . . . . . . 118
- C) The Decretalists . . . . . . . . . . . . 121
- D) A Wide Choice of Writings . . . . . . . . 124
- E) The Study of Canon Law . . . . . . . . . 126
- F) Connection with Moral Theology . . . . . . 127
- G) The Influence of Roman Law . . . . . . . 129

## Third Period
## FROM THE COUNCIL OF TRENT TO THE *CODEX IURIS CANONICI* (1917)

### Chapter I
Foundations of the Development of Canon Law . . . 134

### Chapter II
Documentary Sources . . . . . . . . . . . . 143

  A) Collections of Acts of Popes, Councils, and the Roman Curia . . . . . . . . . . . . . 143
    1. Collections of Papal Acts . . . . . . . 144
    2. Collections of Conciliar Documents . . . . 147
    3. Collections of the Acts of the Roman Curia . . 151
  B) Liturgical Books . . . . . . . . . . . . 151
  C) Attempts at New Codification . . . . . . . 151

### Chapter III
The Science of Law and its Practitioners . . . . . . 155

  A) To 1800 . . . . . . . . . . . . . . . . 155
  B) From 1800 to the *Codex Iuris Canonici* (1917) . . 161

## Fourth Period
## THE *CODEX IURIS CANONICI* OF 1917, ITS COMMENTATORS, AND ITS REVISION IN 1983

### Chapter I
Historical Background and Preparation . . . . . . 165

### Chapter II
The *Codex Iuris Canonici* of 1917 . . . . . . . . . 167

### Chapter III
The *Codex Iuris Canonici* of 1983 . . . . . . . . . 173

# PREFACE

The history of law in general has long held a prominent place at the University of Louvain and, of course, the History of Canon Law occupies a particular place in the Faculty of Canon Law.

Monsignor Alfons Van Hove published his *Prolegomena ad Codicem Iuris Canonici* (1928 and 1945). In this work, he first described the general concepts of law and the constitutive sources of canon law (Parts I-II). He continued with the history of the sources (Part III), and the development of canonical science through the centuries (Part IV). The fifth part concluded with the 1917 lawbook and its commentaries. His work was written in Latin, since canon law was taught in Latin in view of the international character of the Faculty.

Professor Constant Van de Wiel provides what, at first glance, seems to be a reworking of Van Hove's *Prolegomena*, supplemented and improved in the light of later publications. However, his division differs from that of the *Prolegomena*, in which the history of the sources in the various periods was followed by the history of the canonical discipline. Van de Wiel's work offers a twofold improvement. His primary division is that of the periods: a first period runs from the foundation of the Church to the *Decretum Gratiani* (1140), a second from 1140 to the middle of the 16th century, a third from the Council of Trent (1545-1563) to the promulgation of the *Codex Iuris Canonici* (1917), and a fourth from 1917 to the new Codex of 1983. For each of these periods, a brief survey is given of most of the important historical facts or movements that influenced the development of the sources and the systems of canon law (Chapter I), followed by the documentary sources (Chapter II), and a consideration of the science and its practitioners (Chapter III). Thus, the reader is presented with a convenient overview of each period.

The work concludes with a few brief considerations on the new Code, promulgated in 1983, which is not only a revision of the first Code but, indeed, a new code of canon law. Van de Wiel's work is a substantial contribution to the study of the history of canon law and will be of great service especially to students and jurists.

Mgr. W. Onclin<br>
Professor Emeritus of the<br>
Catholic University of<br>
Louvain

Introduction

# CONCEPTS AND TERMS, SOURCES, AND LEGAL DISCIPLINE

1. Canon law is a normative system that includes *canones, decreta, decretalia, constitutiones, praecepta, responsiones, rescripta, epistolae*, and legal customs. In the course of the centuries, however, these terms have been applied to different kinds of legally binding rules, which have been compiled in both private and official collections. Therefore, it is perhaps necessary to introduce the study of these documentary sources and of the history of their origin with a brief historical sketch of the terminology used.

2. "Canon" comes from the Greek word *kanōn* and means, in its proper sense, the stem of a reed and, on that basis, a long and straight piece of wood, a wooden rule used by masons and carpenters, a rule with which straight lines are drawn. Figuratively, it is a rule of the art or of a trade, a model, a type, a definitive list or catalogue. A *mousikos kanōn* is then an instrument that gives the proper pitch to a singer, and the *canon alexandrinus* is the list of the best Greek classical authors, those considered to be the ideal, which was compiled by the grammarians of Alexandria. *Kronikoi kanōnes* are the noteworthy dates that delineate history into eras, while the *canones grammatici* are models of declensions and conjugations and rules of syntax.

3. With the rise of Christianity, *kanōn* received a new meaning: "commandments of God" or, in Latin, *regulae fidei* (truths of faith), and *regulae morum* (behavioral rules). *Kanōn* also indicates the definitive list of the sacred books containing the truths of faith, the moral and liturgical rules, and especially the unchangeable prayer of the consecration and the regulations for priests and monks. *Canonici* can also refer to religious who live according to a rule.

4. It is in this sense of *regulae morum* that "canon" was taken up into law. Although civil laws are also behavioral rules, the word "canon" was, from the outset, used exclusively for Church laws. The Council of Nicea (325), the first of the eight Eastern councils (325-869), used this term for the first time. It speaks of *kanōn ekklēsiastikos* to indicate the totality of disciplinary laws promulgated by the Church. These truths of faith were called *decreta* or *definitiones*. The subsequent Eastern councils also called the disciplinary rules of the Church "canons."

This was to distinguish them from *nomos*, which was used for civil law. When Justinian spoke about the disciplinary measures of the Eastern councils, he also used the word "canon" in opposition to the word *nomos*, the civil law. In the eleventh century, the collections of church laws and civil laws related to church matters were called *collectiones nomocanonum*.

From the early Middle Ages, church laws, that is, the decrees of popes and bishops and the statutes of both general and special councils, were ordinarily called canons. Later, among decretists and decretalists, in the period of greater centralization of the Church, the term canon was increasingly reserved for the decisions of popes and general councils.

The Councils of Basel and Constance in the 15th century called their disciplinary measures "decrees". The Council of Trent (1545-1563) and the First Vatican Council also used this terminology. These councils used "canons" for the truths of faith they proclaimed in the condemnation of heresies. Of course, these canons also had a disciplinary character because of the anathemas.

In the papal acts, the term "canons" was often used to distinguish the universal laws, which were included in the *Corpus Iuris Canonici*, from the decrees of the councils and from the papal constitutions outside the corpus.

The 1917 and 1983 Codes return to the old term: they consist of canons, which contain both disciplinary and dogmatic specifications.

5. From the beginning of the Church, the term *ius canonicum* was used to indicate all of the laws of the Church. This term was

used often throughout the centuries, until it was finally taken up officially in the titles of the 1917 and 1983 Codes. *Ius canonicum* thus indicates all of the rules (*canones, leges*) that are proposed (*propositae*), promulgated (*constitutae*), or approved (*approbatae seu receptae*) by the ecclesiastical authority.

6. Up to the 16th century, the term *ius ecclesiasticum* was widely used along with and as a synonym for *ius canonicum*, to designate all ecclesiastical laws. *Ius ecclesiasticum* concerns the *societas ecclesiastica*, in which the Church is the only source of law. *Ius ecclesiasticum* and *ius canonicum* were used interchangeably.

From the 17th century on, *ius ecclesiasticum* acquired a separate meaning, one introduced by Protestant writers. These understood the expression to mean the laws issued by the civil authorities, in religious matters, on their own initiative and by virtue of a jurisdiction that they had assumed in ecclesiastical affairs.

Later on, the term was used for the body of civil law concerning ecclesiastical matters that was issued by the emperors in virtue of their authority *in sacra*.

In the 19th century and in the beginning of the 20th century, there were three different understandings of the term:

* *Ius canonicum* was synonymous with *ius ecclesiasticum* and indicated the entirety of the Church's own legislation as in the Middle Ages.

* *Ius canonicum* was the law contained in the *Corpus Iuris Canonici; ius ecclesiasticum* was the law of the Church itself after the corpus. Both understandings used the terms *droit civil ecclésiastique, diritto ecclesiastico*, and *Staatskirchenrecht* to describe civil law in ecclesiastical matters.

* *Ius canonicum* was exclusively canon law proper; *ius ecclesiasticum*, however, was the Church's own law as a whole, the civil law in ecclesiastical matters, and concordatory law. Thus, all of *ius canonicum* was *ius eccleciasticum*, but not all *ius ecclesiasticum* was *ius canonicum*.

7. In the 1917 and 1983 Codes, *ius canonicum* is synonymous with *ius ecclesiasticum* and the terms are used interchangeably. They indicate the Church's own law. In practice, however, preference is given to the expression *ius canonicum* to indicate the Church's own law and to *ius ecclesiasticum* for civil law in ecclesiastical matters or for concordatory law. See: R. METZ, "Droit canonique et droit ecclésiastique. Problème de terminologie," *Revue de droit canonique* 29 (1979), p. 37.

8. In Italy, there is no doubt regarding the meaning of *diritto canonico* and *diritto ecclesiastico*. In Germany, the actions of the Nazi regime, which wanted to meddle with doctrinal questions, provoked a reaction from the Catholic Church and, even more so, from the Protestant Church. The two Churches objected to the use of *ius ecclesiasticum* for civil law in ecclesiastical matters, while affirming their own law to be of a theological nature and possessed of a specific character. Therefore, the Germans regard *ius ecclesiasticum* (Kirchenrecht) as equivalent to *ius canonicum*.

In academic circles in Germany, the term *Kanonisches Recht* is now used for law originating from the churches and the term *Kirchenrecht* is synonymous with *Staatskirchenrecht* for civil law affecting the churches. However, the old terminology still survives in *Kirchenrecht*, the law of the churches, and in *Staatsrecht*. Instead of *Staatskirchenrecht*, one speaks of *Katholisches*, *Protestantisches*, or *Evangelisches Kirchenrecht*.

9. *Ius sacrum seu religiosum* was applied in the *Digests of Justinian* (I,1,1) in opposition to the *ius romanum seu saeculare*. *Ius canonicum*, however, contained not only the *sacrum* (consecrated objects) but also the *profanum* (churches, oratories, goods of the church, etc.).

10. *Ius pontificium* or pontifical law, as opposed to imperial law (*ius caesareum*), did not correspond with *ius canonicum* either. Indeed, a bishop, too, could, in principle, according to divine law, issue laws for his diocese. Moreover, ecumenical councils have legislative power for the entire Church; plenary, national, and

provincial councils have such power for a part of the Church (conciliar law). Every religious institute, moreover, creates regular law for its members, and the apostolic vicars and prefects issue missionary law. Regular and missionary law can also be called pontifical, because they are created by delegates of the pope. The law that these various authorities issue is covered by the term *ius canonicum*.

11. After the eleventh century we find *ius decretalium* or decretal law because decretals became the most important source of canon law.

12. The word "sources" has a double meaning. Ecclesiastical rules are known to us from documentary sources. (See no. 19 below). The legal authority from which the laws proceed, to which they owe their origin (*causae effectivae*), are the constitutive sources, the *ius divinum* and the *ius positivum humanum*.

13. Divine Law (*ius divinum*)

a) The primary lawgiver is God. God promulgated the *ius divinum positivum*. It consists of what God has made known by means of revelation or the Holy Scripture and is contained in the Old Testament. Distinct from this is the *ius divinum naturale*, "*non scripta, sed nata lex*" (Cicero), or the laws that are obvious (*naturale*) to every reasonable being.

b) In addition, Jesus Christ, the founder and supreme lawgiver of the Church, has also proclaimed a *ius divinum positivum*, contained in the New Testament and Tradition.

Natural law and divine law are correlative; they exist in harmony. Divine law only completes and specifies the data of natural law, which itself is of divine origin. The Church, therefore, cannot bypass natural law. (See C.I.C. 1983, can. 199, 1°, 1163 § 2, 1165 § 2, 1259, 1299 § 1; cf. Y. Congar, "Jus divinum," *Revue de droit canonique* 28 (1978), pp. 108-122). The Church derives its laws from the *ius divinum*, which it, in fact, only presents and interprets. Thus, one speaks of *ius propositum* as the first source of law in the Church.

14. Positive Human Law (*ius positivum humanum*)

c) The Apostles received from Jesus Christ the power to issue laws for the universal Church. They are contained in Scripture (primarily the Epistles) and Tradition.

d) The bishops, as successors to the Apostles, derive their collegial legislative power directly from divine law.

The Pope, as Bishop of Rome and the successor of Peter, receives, from Scripture and Tradition, the primacy of honor and jurisdiction over the entire Church. From the beginning of the third century, the bishops of Southern and Central Italy turned directly to the Pope. From the end of the fourth century, the Pope also intervened in the East. He gave advice, drew up rules of behavior, resolved disputes, and issued judgments. The oldest decretal known to us is the letter *Dominus inter* of Pope Damasus (366-384) to the bishops of Gaul, in which he stated the conditions for becoming a priest. In 385 Pope Siricius (384-399) replied to Bishop Himerus of Tarragone regarding questions previously posed to Pope Damasus. In the course of the fifth century, the popes no longer limited themselves to the resolution of concrete difficulties, but, on their own initiative, issued general norms for an entire region, for example, Gaul or Africa. The Pope is thus, in law and in fact, the bishop of the Catholic world. During the Middle Ages and in early modern times, this trend continued. Problems were presented to him not only from European Christianity but also from the world discovered since Christopher Columbus.

Therefore, it is essential for canonists to know the names of the Roman interventions. Today the terminology continues to be very confused: *epistulae, litterae, encyclicae, responsa, sententiae, rescripta* (of private interest), *constitutiones* (of general interest), *decreta, decretales, chirographi* (from the hand of the Pope himself), *monita, bullae, motu proprio, instructiones*, and *declarationes* all refer to documents of a more or less authoritative nature that come either from the Pope or from one of the Roman congregations or dicasteries. (See: P. ANDRIEU-GUITRANCOURT, *Introduc-*

*tion sommaire à l'étude du droit en général et du droit canonique contemporain en particulier*, Paris, 1963, p. 583.)

The Second Vatican Council (11 October 1962 - 8 December 1965) used a strict terminology for its sixteen documents, dividing them into three groups.

First, there are the documents with an essential doctrinal content. These are the constitutions: *Sacrosanctum Concilium* of December 4, 1963, on the liturgy; *Lumen Gentium* of November 21, 1964, on the church; *Dei Verbum* of November 18, 1965, on Revelation; *Gaudium et spes* of December 7, 1965, on the Church in the world. Texts of a more practical nature and of more concrete application were contained in nine decrees: *Unitatis redintegratio* of November 21, 1964, on ecumenism; *Inter mirifica* of December 4, 1964, on the means of social communication; *Orientalium ecclesiarum* of December 21, 1964, on the Eastern Catholic Churches; *Christus Dominus* of October 28, 1965, on the pastoral mission of the bishops; *Apostolicam actuositatem* of November 18, 1965, on the apostolate of the laity; *Perfectae caritatis* of November 28, 1965, on the renewal and adaptation of religious life; Optatam totius Ecclesiae of November 28, 1965, on the training of priests; *Presbyterorum ordinis* of December 7, 1965, on the life and ministry of priests; *Ad Gentes* of December 7, 1965, on the Missionary activity of the Church.

The term "declaration" was used for the first time during the Second Vatican Council. It indicates texts directed to the people, believers and non-believers, to whom the Church declares (*declarat*) its point of view on questions of general concern. These are: *Nostra aetate* of October 28, 1965, on the relations of the Church with other non-Christian religions (particularly with Judaism); *Gravissimum educationis* of October 28, 1965, on Christian education; *Dignitatis humanae* of December 7, 1965, on religious freedom.

The general or ecumenical councils (all the bishops under the leadership of the pope) legislate for the entire Church because they, together (*collegialiter*) and by virtue of their function (*ordo episcoporum*), care for the universal church community.

The first eight ecumenical councils were held in the East, and twenty-one have been held in all up to the present. Councils only became possible after the Peace of Constantine in 313. Their principal objective was to condemn heresy, but they also issued disciplinary measures.

Bishops, united in a plenary (for several ecclesiastical provinces), provincial, or national council (for their province or nation), legislate for the area over which they have jurisdiction.

The individual bishops are, by virtue of divine law, appointed to their particular churches to administer them under the authority of the pope with ordinary jurisdiction (*potestas ordinaria propria*) (C.I.C. 1983, can. 381 and 391).

They administer their dioceses personally in the name of Christ and participate in the collective jurisdictional power of all bishops (*ordo episcoporum*). (Cf. P. Anciaux, "L'épiscopat (ordo episcoporum) comme réalité sacramentelle," *Nouvelle Revue Théologique* 85 (1963), pp. 139-159.)

Territorial prelates and abbots, apostolic prefects, apostolic vicars, and apostolic administrators enjoy the same faculty. They administer a mission area or diocese in the name of the pope (*potestas ordinaria vicaria*). This is also the case for the cathedral chapter *sede vacante* and the chapter vicar, who must be appointed within eight days by the chapter and who administer the diocese temporarily in the name of the chapter. These faculties were transferred in the new Code to a college of consultors, which names an episcopal administrator within eight days (can. 421 § 1). According to the new Code, the administrator has the same rights as the former chapter vicar. Their prescriptions are true laws and are called statutes and sometimes also decrees. They are decreed by the meeting of the bishop and the various prominent clerics of the diocese united in a synod.

The word decree is also used in another sense, i.e., the enforcement of laws or the imposition of sanctions; for example, decrees on the occasion of a diocesan visitation or the visitation of a religious community and decrees issued by judges (sentences, intermediary decrees).

e) The general chapters of institutes of consecrated life, societies of apostolic life and their provincial chapters — the latter only in matters stipulated by the constitutions — have legislative power.

In addition to the legislative power of these institutes, cathedral chapters *sede plena*, pious associations, and confraternities, which have the purpose of practising acts of piety or charity and/or promoting public cult, and universities —according to the most common opinion—have no legislative power, but only the authority to draw up conventional statutes. However, they must be approved by the local ordinary (in the case of confraternities and pious associations) or the Holy See (in the case of universities) and cannot be amended without their permission. Yet even with this approval they do not acquire the status of a law. For example, the prescriptions imposed by the bishop on the chapter are true laws but the statutes of the chapter, which are only approved by the bishop, are not.

f) A concordat is an agreement between the ecclesiastical and the civil authority to regulate matters that concern them. Every concordat constitutes both civil and canon law for a specific territory. A concordatory regime presumes that the state recognizes the Church as a sovereign power and thus as a true society and not merely as a private association.

On the Church's side, the negotiators are the Holy See for the universal Church, and the bishops for their territory and in matters over which they have free decision-making power. In practice, usually only the Holy see concludes concordats because these often change the general law, treat mostly of matters reserved to the Holy See like marriage, the liturgy, the establishment of new dioceses, etc., and apply for an entire nation, which can consist of several dioceses.

The head of state (emperor, king, or president) or the government negotiates for the state.

Concordats deal with such things as the rights and freedoms of the Church, the establishment, dissolution, and delineation of dioceses, education, marriage, ecclesiastical property rights (alienation, taxes), support of houses of worship and the clergy, immunities, and the election of bishops. Dissolution occurs by mutual agreement, upon by the expiration of a specified period of time, or by grave and unacceptable violation of the agreement by one of the parties. It can also be broken if it was concluded under force or by deceit, if conditions have changed to such an extent that it would never have been concluded under those conditions, or if the state has undergone a fundamental reform.

The law that the Church forms in this way, either at its own initiative (c-e) (canon law proper) or in collaboration with the civil authorities (f) (concordatory law), is the *ius constitutum*.

g) Civil laws, insofar as they are canonized, also form a constituent element of positive canon law. Thus, prescriptions from Belgian law were recognized in the 1983 Code, for example, concerning contracts, can. 1290, cf. can. 1529 CIC 1917; prescription, can. 197 and 1268, cf. can. 1508 CIC 1917; amicable settlement and arbitration, can. 1714 and 1716, cf. can. 1926 and 1930 CIC 1917; adoption as impediment to marriage, can. 1094, cf. can. 1059 and 1080 CIC 1917; possessory actions, can. 1500, cf. 1693-1700 CIC 1917; conditions of the validity of wills, can. 1299 §2, cf. can. 1513 §2 CIC 1917; administration of church property, can. 1284 §1, 1° and 2°, cf. can. 1523, no. 2. Cf. P. Ciprotti, "Le 'leggi civili' nel nuovo Codice di diritto canonico," *Apollinaris* 57 (1984), pp. 281-293. The secular law thus taken up in Church law and approved is called *ius receptum seu approbatum*.

15. In addition to the constitutive or "material" (to use German terminology) sources, the Church accepted civil law as supplementary until the promulgation of the 1917 Code. Canon 20, which expressly deals with the *ius suppletivum*, no longer mentions civil law. Neither does Canon 19 of the Code of 1983 refer to civil law as a source of supplementary law. Insofar as the stipulations of civil law can still be useful for the Church, they are explicitly taken up in the Code.

16. Are the writings of the Fathers - the list was concluded in the West with Gregory the Great († 604) or, better, with Isidore of Seville († 636), and in the East with John Damascene († 749) - constitutive sources of canon law?

For the West, the four great Church Fathers and Doctors are Ambrose (339-397), Jerome (347-419/420), Augustine (354-430), and Gregory the Great (590-604); for the East: Athanasius (295-373), Basil (ca. 330-379), Gregory Nazianzen (329/330-390), and John Chrysostom (ca. 350-407).

The Western Church has never granted the force of law even to positions unanimously held by the Fathers of the Church. Nevertheless, the Fathers are considered to be the most complete transmitters and reliable interpreters of the teaching of the Apostles. The Fathers established liturgical and moral rules on the basis of apostolic teaching. In this sense, their writings formed an authoritative source of canon law, but not a constitutive or legislative source. Nonetheless they were a source of inspiration for the legislators of the time. Because the Fathers and Doctors were generally at the head of a diocese or monastery, they had practical experience and could therefore decide principles for the administration of the Christian communities. Hence, they continue to be important witnesses of the discipline then applicable and of the law of the Church, both universal and particular.

Nevertheless, in the East and, more particularly, in the Greek Orthodox Church, the writings of the Fathers have been recognized as having the force of law from the sixth century onwards.

Cf. A. HAMMAN, *Les pères de l'Eglise*, Paris, 1977 (= ID., *Guide pratique des Pères de l'Eglise*, Paris, 1977; ID., *Dictionnaire des Pères de l'Eglise*, Paris, 1977; B. ALTANER-A. STUIBER, *Patrologie. Leben, Schriften und Lehre der Kirchenväter*, Freiburg-Basel-Wien, 1978[8]; G. PETERS, *Lire les Pères de l'Église. Cours de patrologie*, Paris, 1981, 784p.; J. QUASTEN, *Patrology*, vols I-III, Westminster, 1988, vol. IV, Edited by A. di Berfardino, Westminster, 1988[2].

17. The writings of ecclesiastical writers such as Clement of Alexandria († can 216), Origen (ca. 185-ca. 254), Irenaeus (ca. 130-ca. 200), Tertullian (160-222/3), Lactantius (before 250-ca. 323), Eusebius of Caesarea († can 340) do not form a constituent

source of canon law. Nevertheless, they bear witness of the laws, customs, and institutions of their time.

Even the writings of eminent scholars of the Middle Ages and of the Early Modern Times, which were proclaimed *doctores Ecclesiae* by the Church are included in Church law. These teachers include among others: Bernard (1090-1153), Anthony of Padua (ca. 1190/1195-1231), Thomas Aquinas (1225/1226-1274), Bonaventure (1221-1274), Theresa of Avila (1515-1582), John of the Cross (1542-1591), Francis de Sales (1567-1622), and Alphonse of Liguori (1669-1787).

18. Roman congregations and the dicasteries cannot legislate on their own. With the approval of the Pope, they can issue official interpretations of laws, make executive decisions, and even draft new prescriptions insofar as the Code has not provided some. Constant jurisprudence of the ecclesiastical tribunals, even that of the Roman Rota, is not considered to be a source of ecclesiastical legislation either. The importance of the prescriptions of the Roman congregations, dicasteries, and ecclesiastical tribunals, however, makes them an essential source of the legislative process.

19. These various laws are collected and preserved in two ways. An authentic compilation is made on the order of a lawful authority, which later approves and promulgates them. This rarely occurs. The compilations made by private initiative have no legal character. Each document included in them retains its own individual value. Exceptionally, some private collections partially took on the force of law in time, such as some volumes of the *Decretum Gratiani*.

Because these collections compile the law, they are called documentary sources of law (*fontes cognoscitivi, fontes scientiae*, or *cognitionis iuris*). The Germans call them formal sources.

Alongside the strictly juridical works, there are also numerous editions of writings of the Fathers, ecclesiastical writers, and Doctors of the Church, the importance of which we have already stressed. From the seventeenth century on, they have been examined critically. Such a collection was published in Paris by the French priest, Jacques Paul Migne (1800-1875) under the title *Patrologiae cursus completus*. The *series latina* (PL) contains the Latin writers from Tertullian († 222/3) through Innocent III († 1216) in 222 volumes (1844-1864) and was supplemented by a *Patrologiae cursus completus, Series Latina, supplementum* by A. Hamman, 5 volumes, Paris, 1958-1974. The *Series Graeca (series Graece-latina)* (PG) contains the Greek fathers from Saint Barnabas (+ ca. 60) to the council of Florence (1439) in 167 volumes, 1857-1866. The *Series Graeca et Orientalis. Patrologia Graeca. Latine tantum edita* contains 85 volumes, 1856-1867. Cf. A.G. Hamman, *Jacques Paul Migne. Le retour aux Pères de l'Eglise* (coll. *Le point théologique*, 16), Paris, 1975; "Centenaire Jacques Paul Migne," (1875-1975), *Sacris Erudiri*, 22 (1974-1975), 1-111; A. Mandouze-J. Fouilheron (eds.), *Migne et le renouveau des études patristiques (Actes du colloque de Saint-Flour*, 7-8 July 1975); *Théologie historique*, 66, Paris, 1985.

The *Patrologia Latina* also contains canonical compilations such as the collection of canons and decretals of Dionysius Exiguus (vol. 67, cols. 139-346); Book 5 *de legibus et temporibus* from the *Etymologiarum libri viginti* (vol. 82, cols. 198-228) by Isidore Hispalensis; *de ecclesiasticis officiis*, by Isidore of Seville (vol. 83, cols. 738-826); canons of Greek, African, French, and Spanish councils, decretals of 20 popes, namely from Damasus I (366-384) to Gregory the Great (590-604) (vol. 84); the *Liber Diurnus Romanorum Pontificum* (vol. 105, cols. 9-187); the *Pseudo-Isidorianae* (vol. 130); the *Decretorum libri XX* of Burchard of Worms (vol. 140, cols. 537-1066); and the *Decretum* and the *Panormia* of Yves of Chartres (vol. 161).

A critical and supplemented edition of Migne's work has been published in three parts under the title *Corpus Christianorum: Series Latina* (first eight centuries to the Venerable Bede) beginning in 1953; the *Series Graeca* beginning in 1977; the *Continuatio mediaevalis* (from the eighth to the twelfth century) beginning in 1966. Each volume contains an introduction, an updated bibliography, critical apparatus, and an index. The Benedictine

Abbey of Steenbrugge (Belgium) began this project in 1945 and is still directing it. In the *Corpus Christianorum, series Latina,* the *Concilia Galliae a. 314-695* is contained in vol. 148, (1963) and the *Concilia Africae a. 345-525* in vol. 149 (1974). The *Collectio canonum in V libris (lib. I-III)* was published in the *Continuatio mediaevalis* in vol. 6, 1 (1970) and *De computu* of Rabanus Maurus in vol. 44 (1979).

For the texts of the oriental Fathers we have a collection in the *Corpus Scriptorum Christianorum Orientalium* (CSCO). This series was founded in 1903 by the professors Jean-Baptiste Chabot of Louvain and Hubert Hyvernat of Washington, and continued by René Draguet in 1948. It still produces some ten volumes yearly (for 1988, Vols. 497-506).

20. The science of canon law or *scientia iuris canonici,* is practiced by the *doctores* or *scriptores (iuris canonici),* which, grouped in schools, have different methodologies. They create no law because they are neither legislators nor judges. They strive to provide a justified systematization of law by analysis, ordering, and classification and thus construct a science of law.

21. Bibliography

*- Canones, ius canonicum*

A. VAN HOVE, *Prologomena,* nos. 39, 40, 41, 44-75, 110-111.
M. LALMANT, art. "Canon," *Dictionnaire de droit canonique,* vol. II, 1937, col. 1283-1288.
R. NAZ, art. "Droit canonique," in *Dictionnaire de droit canonique,* vol. IV, 1949, col. 1446-1495.
R. METZ, "Droit canonique et droit ecclésiastique. Problème de terminologie," *Revue de droit canonique* 29 (1979), pp. 23-40.
P. LOMBARDIA, "La relación entre Derecho canónico y Derecho eclesiástico," *Ius canonicum* 22 (1982), pp. 11-30.

*- Concordata*

H. WAGNON, *Concordats et droit international. Fondement, élaboration, valeur et cessation du droit concordataire,* Gembloux, 1935, XXVIII - 441 p.

R. NAZ, art. "Concordat," *Dictionnaire de droit canonique*, vol. III, 1942, col. 1353-1383.

R. MINNERATH, *L'Eglise et les Etats concordataires (1846-1981), La souveraineté spirituelle*, Paris, 1983.

## 22. General Bibliography

### 1. Monographs

F. MAASEN, *Geschichte der Quellen und der Literatur des canonischen Rechts im Abendlande bis zum Ausgange des Mittelalters*, Graz, 1870 (anastatic reprint, Graz, 1956).

J. F. von SCHULTE, *Die Geschichte der Quellen und Literatur des canonischen Rechts von Gratian bis auf die Gegenwart*, 3 vols., Stuttgart, 1875-1880 (anastatic reprint, Graz, 1956).

A. TARDIF, *Histoire des sources du droit canonique*, Paris, 1887 (anastatic reprint, Aalen, 1974).

H. HURTER, *Nomenclator literarius theologiae catholicae*, vol. I, Innsbruck, 1926[4]; vol. II-VI, Innsbruck, 1903-1913[3] (anastatic reprint, New York, 1962).

U. CHEVALIER, *Répertoire des sources historiques du Moyen Age, Bio-Bibliographie*, 2 vols., Paris, 1905-1907[2] (anastatic reprint, New York, 1960).

F. CIMETIER, *Les sources du droit ecclésiastique*, Paris, 1930.

P. FOURNIER - G. LE BRAS, *Histoire des collections canoniques en Occident depuis les fausses décrétales jusqu'au décret de Gratien*, Paris, 1931-1932 (anastatic reprint, Aalen, 1972).

S. KUTTNER, *Repertorium der kanonistik (1140-1234), Prodromus corporis glossarum I*, Città del Vaticano, 1937 (anastatic reprint, Rome, 1972, Modena, 1981).

A. VAN HOVE, *Prolegomena ad Codicem iuris canonici*, Malines-Rome, 1945[2] (anastatic reprint, Malines, 1959).

B. KURTSCHEID - F. WILCHES, *Historia iuris canonici*, I: *Historia fontium et scientiae iuris canonici*, Rome, 1948[2].

A. STICKLER, *Historia iuris canonici latini*, I: *Historia fontium*, Turin, 1950 (second anastatic reprint, Rome, 1985).

W. M. PLÖCHL, *Geschichte des Kirchenrechts*, 5 Vols., Vienna-Munich, vol. I, 1960[2]; vol. II, 1962[2]; vol. III, 1970[2]; vol. IV, 1966; vol. V, 1969.

CH. MUNIER, *Les sources patristiques du droit de l'Eglise du 8e au 13e siécle*, Mulhouse, 1957.

P. ANDRIEU - GUITRANCOURT, *Introduction sommaire à l'étude du droit en général et du droit canonique contemporain en particulier*, Paris, 1963.

A. Garcia y Garcia, *Historia del Derecho Canonico*, vol. I: *El primer Milenio*, Salamanca, 1967.
Tusculum Lexikon, *Griechischer und lateinischer Autoren des Altertums und des Mittelalters*, Munich, 1982³.
H. E. Feine, *Kirchliche Rechtsgeschichte*, vol. 1: *Die katholische Kirche*, Cologne-Vienna, 1972⁵.
H. Coing, *Handbuch der Quellen und Literatur der neueren europäischen Privatrechtsgeschichte*, vol. I: *Mittelalter (1100-1500)*, Munich, 1973, pp. 39-397; vol. II: *Neuere Zeit (1500-1800)*, Munich, 1976-1977; vol. III: *Das 19. Jahrhundert*, Munich, 1982-1987.
A. Pietro, "El proceso del formacion del derecho canonico," cap. II, *Derecho canonico*, Pamplona, 1975, pp. 89-138. Translation in Italian: "Il processo di formazione del diritto canonico," cap. II, *Corso di diritto canonico*, P. I, Turin, 1975, pp. 75-124.
J. A. Clarence Smith, *Medieval Law Teachers and Writers, Civilian and Canonist*, Ottawa, 1975.
W. Ullmann, *Law and Politics in the Middle Ages*, London, 1975.
A. Giacobbi, "Il diritto nella storia della Chiesa, Sintesi di storia delle fonti e delle istituzioni," *Il diritto nel mistero della Chiesa*, I, *Introduzione*, Rome, 1979, pp. 117-236.
*Introduction bibliographique à l'histoire du droit et à l'ethnologie juridique*, Brussels, vol. B, nr 9: J. Gaudemet, *Droit canonique* (1963); nr. 10: R. Feenstra, *Droit romain au Moyen Age (1100-1500)* (1979).
J. Dahyot-Dolivet, *Précis d'histoire du droit canonique. Fondement et évolution*, Rome, 1984.
G. May - A. Egler, *Die Geschichte der Kirchenrechtswissenschaft*, in *Einführung in die Kirchenrechtliche Methode*, Regensburg, 1986, pp. 37-104.

2. Encyclopedia

*Dictionnaire de théologie catholique*, 15 vols., Paris, 1903-1950; vol. 16: *Tables générales*, 1951-1972.
*Dictionnaire d'histoire et de géographie ecclésiastiques*, Paris, 1912-
*Dictionnaire d'archéologie chrétienne et de liturgie*, 15 vols., Paris, 1907-1953.
*Dictionnaire de droit canonique*, 7 vols., Paris, 1935-1965.
*Encyclopédie du catholicisme*, Paris, 1948-
*Enciclopedia cattolica*, 12 vols., Città del Vaticano, 1948-1954.
*Lexikon für Theologie und Kirche*, 11 vols., Freiburg im Breisgau, 1957-1967². *Concilium Vaticanum II*, 3 vols., 1966-1968.
*New Catholic Encyclopedia*, 17 vols., New York, 1967-1979.
*Novissimo Digesto Italiano*, 20 vols., Turin, 1957-1975 (anastatic reprint, Turin, 1974-1976, 7 suppl. 1980-1987).

## 3. Periodicals and Series

*L'année canonique*, Paris, 1952-
*Apollinaris. Commentarius Instituti Utriusque Iuris*, Rome, 1928-
*Archiv für katholisches Kirchenrecht*, Innsbruck - Mainz, 1857-
*Bulletin of Medieval Canon Law. New Series*, Berkeley, California, 1971-
*Les cahiers de droit ecclésial*, Luçon, 1984-
*Canon Law Abstracts. A Half-yearly Review of Periodical Literature in Canon Law*, Dygrange - Melrose, Edinburgh, 1959-
*Commentarium pro religiosis et missionariis*, Roma, 1935- (continuation of *Commentarium pro religosis*, 1920-1934).
*Communicationes. Pontificia commissio Codici iuris canonici recognoscendo*, Rome, 1969-
*Il diritto ecclesiastico*, Rome, 1926 (continuation of *Rivista di diritto ecclesiastico*, 1890-1925).
*Ephemerides iuris canonici*, Rome, 1945-
*Ephemerides theologicae lovanienses*, Louvain, 1924-
*The Jurist*, Washington, 1941-
*Ius canonicum*, Pamplona, 1961-
*Kanon. Jahrbuch der Gesellschaft für das Recht der Ostkirchen. Yearbook of the Society of the Law of the Oriental Churches. Annuaire de la Société du droit des Eglises Orientales*, Vienna, 1973-
*Monitor ecclesiasticus*, Rome, 1940- (continuation of *Il monitore ecclesiastico*, 1876-1939).
*Münchener theologische Studien, Kanonistische Abteilung*, Munich, 1951-
*Österreichisches Archiv für Kirchenrecht*, Vienna, 1950-
*Periodica de re morali, canonica, liturgica*, Rome, 1927- (continuation of *De religiosis... periodica*, 1905- ), and of *Periodica de re canonica et morali*, 1920-1926).
*Praxis juridique et religion*, Strasbourg, 1984-
*Proceedings of the International Congresses of Medieval Canon Law*, in *Monumenta iuris canonici. Series C: subsidia*, 1965-
*Review of Religious*, Saint Louis, Missouri, 1942-
*Revista Española de derecho canonico*, Madrid, 1946-
*Revue de droit canonique*, Strasbourg, 1951-
*Studia canonica. Revue canadienne de droit canonique (A Canadian Law Review)*, Ottawa, 1967-
*Studia et documenta historiae et iuris*, Rome, 1935-
*Studia Gratiana*, Bononia - Rome, 1953-
*Zeitschrift für Evangelisches Kirchenrecht*, Tubingen, 1951-
*Zeitschrift der Savigny-Stiftung für Rechtsgeschichte, Kanonistische Abteilung*, Weimar, 1911-

FIRST PERIOD
# FROM THE FOUNDATION OF THE CHURCH TO GREGORY VII (1073-1085)

## Chapter I

## HISTORICAL FRAMEWORK

23. Because of their mission, the Apostles traveled everywhere throughout the Mediterranean area, founding Christian communities and putting men in charge of them. Thus, Paul visited Asia Minor, Greece, Rome, and probably also Spain. Peter founded the Christian community in Rome from which the seat of the supreme authority developed.

The Roman emperors, however, feared that their state religion would be replaced by the new faith, which could threaten their own political power. Therefore, many of them were not sympathetic to the new Church and decided to persecute it. Of those persecutions which the first Christians suffered, the most severe were those under Nero (54-68), Domitian (81-96), Trajan (98-117), Decius (249-251), and Diocletian (284-305). Only the conversion of Constantine the Great in 312 brought an end to this cruel suppression. Christians could openly confess their faith and celebrate their liturgy. Gradually, small communities were formed, which constituted a kind of diaspora in a pagan environment.

The impulse towards expansion and self-government of these local churches is reflected in a number of documents on the organization of the believing community and the prescriptions for a Christian life in conformity with Tradition. These sources, which date from the first three centuries, generally originated in the East. They have been gathered together with the apostolic and pseudo-apostolic writings. An important part of the text collections of the Eastern Churches (Greece, Asia Minor) from before the Council of Nicea (325) deal with ecclesiastical discipline.

24. In the fourth and fifth centuries, the Roman Empire was divided into two territories: the Eastern Roman Empire and the Western Roman Empire.

A) The Church in the Eastern Roman Empire.

The conversion of Emperor Constantine (ca. 280-306-337) to Christianity in 312 ushered in a completely new era, not only for the Roman state but also for the young Church.

Constantine and Licinius, Emperor of the West (+324) granted Christians freedom of religion with the Edict of Milan in 313. This involved recognition of the right to be a Christian and restitution of church goods that had been seized. The official pagan cult, however, and the other cults were left undisturbed. The emperors granted the priests of the new religion the same exemption from public and personal charges that the pagan cult leaders enjoyed.

After 321, the Church could receive legates, and it was given the right to observe Sunday rest. Constantine elevated the new religion to the status of state religion and from then on recognized the Christian communities as juridical persons.

In 313, Constantine donated the Lateran Palace to the Pope. Around 320, he laid the first stone of St. Peter's Basilica above the tomb of St. Peter on the Vatican Hill. Shortly thereafter, he started building the Basilica of the Holy Sepulchre in Jerusalem. The basilica in Christ's birthplace, Bethlehem, and the double church in the imperial palace in Trier were constructed gradually.

When Licinius died in 324, Constantine became the sole ruler of the entire Roman empire. A year later, he summoned all the bishops of his empire to the general Council of Nicea (325), the first ecumenical council, to resolve the theological disputes that had arisen. This council restored the unity of the Church.

In 330, Constantine gave the empire a new capital. Rome had too pagan a character. The empire was expanding in the East and Constantine moved his administrative headquarters to Byzantium on the Bosporus, the connecting point between Europe and Asia. He named the new capital after himself, Constantinople, and crowned the city with an immense basilica, the Hagia Sophia, the church of the One God or the Three in One (cf. Eusebius, *Vita Constantini*).

The sons of Constantine continued his policy. They fought superstition and forbade pagan sacrifices (341). The emperors Gratian (West, 375-383) and Theodosius (East, 379-388) — the Empire had been divided — made Christianity the only legitimate religion. Every unorthodox Christian cult was prohibited and persecuted.

By the decree *Cunctos populos* of 380, the emperors declared that only those who confessed the doctrine of the Trinity were Catholic Christians. All others were "maniacs and fools." As heretics, they would incur the imperial wrath. This same prescription introduced the *Codex Justiniani* (C. I,I,1). Justinian (527-565) considered himself the head of the Church and of the State and thus appropriated to himself both ecclesiastical and civil authority. His meddling extended even to ecclesiastical affairs and to problems of faith and dogma. In exchange for this, he and his successors granted to the Church, as the state religion, preferential treatment in numerous areas. The church received subsidies, exemption from certain taxes and services, and jurisdiction. Various measures led to a recognition of the *privilegium fori* and the ecclesiastical right of asylum.

In subsequent decades, the Eastern Roman or Byzantine empire withstood the invasions of the Slavic peoples and thus cast itself as defender of Christianity. In the first five centuries, several councils were convened. They resulted in a considerable number of decisions. They were all the more important because the eastern part of the Roman empire dominated the declining West both ecclesiastically and politically. Up to the fifteenth century, Roman law, with the entire *Corpus Iuris Civilis* of Justinian as its source, endured and continued to be applicable under the name of Byzantine or late-Roman law.

B) The Church in the Western Roman Empire

In the West, things evolved quite differently. In the fourth century, some Germanic tribes had settled in the Western Roman Empire. Great masses of "barbarians" took it by surprise in the fifth century. Ultimately, it collapsed under that pressure in 476. In that year Odoaker (434-493), leader of the Germans in Italy, removed Romulus Augustulus, the last Western Roman emperor, and for some time thereafter he succeeded in withstanding the aspirations of Constantinople. When he was assassinated by Theodoric the Great (456-499-526) in 493, the Empire came under the dominance of the Ostrogoths. After the death of Theodoric, the empire disintegrated into several states. These developed as independent kingdoms.

The bellicosity and conquests of the "barbarians" were accompanied by a drive to destroy Roman culture and civilization. In calm periods, however, they respected and appreciated the cultural achievements of the Romans. Their openness to Roman civilization allowed them to assimilate it to a large degree, partially because of the Church, which clung fast to this higher civilization. Although the Church did lose its protector when the empire disappeared, it became more independent of the state.

From the beginning of the great migrations, the Church set out to convert the Germanic and Slavic peoples. At the same time, it strove to introduce the culture of classical antiquity among them. The conversion of Clovis at the end of the fifth century promoted the merger of the Germanic world with the cultures of Christian-classical antiquity. By uniting a Christian faith and a Christian culture, the Church created an opportunity for spreading the faith in the West. In exchange for this, the privileges and favors already received from Constantine were expanded. The churches were richly endowed with goods, and bishops obtained, among other things, a major role in the administration of the country.

The Church was able to set itself above the converted Germanic kings. This, of course, would have been inconceivable with respect to the Roman emperors. All of this remained restricted to national churches under royal authority, independent of Rome. Some kings were even hostile to the papacy, Thus, the Longobards, who invaded Italy in 568 and established a kingdom in the North (568-774), did not at all approve of the Pope's laying claim to his own state in central Italy. Although there were still too many obstacles to universal unity or a papal supremacy, we note already in the Early Middle Ages signs and claims that could lead to a centralization in Rome.

Already in the fourth century, the popes considered that they were entitled to priority and leadership (cf. the Edict of Milan, 313). Ambrose († 397) and Augustine († 430) were convinced that the Church could claim supremacy over the state. According to St. Augustine, the Christian Emperor is the son of the Church, and the Church, as the *City of God* in becoming, stands above the *City of Man*.

Pope Leo I the Great (440-461) left no doubt that the Bishop of Rome also had the right to primacy over the Church in the East, although the East simply did not accept it. Justinian and his successors regarded the papacy as one of the patriarchates of the Empire. In fact, little attention was paid to the legates of the Western popes. Moreover, the popes were themselves strongly under the influence of Byzantium until the eighth century. Often they were from the East, and held to the Greek-Christian culture.

According to Pope Gelasius I (492-496), there were two autonomous monarchies: one secular (*regalis potestas*) and one spiritual (*auctoritas sacrata pontificia*), independent of one another. Although each had authority in its own area, the center of gravity was still with the spiritual power, because kings ultimately have to account for their actions to God.

St. Boniface (675-754), a missionary north of the Rhine, sent regular reports of his activities to Rome. Together with Pepin the Short (741-768), King of the Franks, he worked for a reorganization of the hierarchy, the reinstitution of discipline among the clergy, and the return to the Church of property taken from or out of the Church.

When Pepin granted Pope Stephan II (752-757) secular authority over large areas of Central Italy in 754, his action involved implicit recognition, at least morally, of the superiority of the Pope. By the confirmation of the *donatio Pepini* in 756, the Pope was able to effectively establish his primacy over the Church.

The *donatio Constantini* (between 750 and 760), which was found to be inauthentic in the fifteenth century, was even more emphatic: not only had the pope received the Lateran palace, but Constantine, in this "official" act, had also granted him supreme civil and ecclesiastical authority over the West.

In the second half of the eighth century, the Frankish Empire underwent a cultural renewal, the Carolingian Renaissance. The Church, too, was part of it. In the person of Charlemagne (768-814), the Church thought it recognized a faithful follower of the pope and a true defender of the Roman religion. Indeed, he subjected the Longobards to the Pope, to whom he gave secular authority over Rome and the Exarchate of Ravenna as independent jurisdictions. In order to revive Christian life, Charlemagne promulgated imperial laws in ecclesiastical matters and organized imperial synods. For these reasons, Pope Leo III (795-816) anointed him emperor and thus appointed him defender of Western Christianity as the successor of the Roman emperor.

For the Pope, the coronation meant that he, as spiritual leader and vicar of Christ, transmitted secular power to Charlemagne. Charlemagne, however, saw things differently. The problem that would overshadow the Western political stage for the coming three centuries had taken concrete form: the struggle between Pope and emperor for supremacy was irreparably launched.

The son of Charlemagne, Louis the Pious (814-840), still provided strong support for the Church. The inevitable division of the empire after Louis' death in 843 meant an obscure period of powerlessness and decline for the Church. The pope became the toy of powerful Italian families. Only in the middle of the eleventh century would the Church begin to recover and emerge from the "dark era of the Middle Ages" (Ceasar Baronius, † 1607). This resulted in what would become in Europe, after the eleventh century, the one Christian society under the supreme administration of the pope.

Bibliography

F. CALLAEY, *Praelectiones historiae ecclesiasticae antiquae*, Rome, 1962[4].
H. LIETZMANN, *A History of Early Church*, vol. I, London, 1974[2]; vol. II, London, 1967[3].
D. HEGGELBACHER, *Geschichte des frühchristlichen Kirchenrechts bis zum Konzil von Nizäa 325*, Freiburg, 1974.
K. BAUS, *Von der Urgemeinde zur frühchristlichen Grosskirche*, Vol. I: H. JEDIN (ed.), *Handbuch der Kirchengeschichte*, Freiburg-Basel-Vienna, 1978[3].
M. WOJTOWYTSCH, "Papsttum und Konzile von den Anfängen bis zu Leo I (440-461)," *Päpste und Papsttum*, vol. 17, Stuttgart, 1981.
K. F. MORRISON, *The Church in the Roman Empire*, vol. 3, Readings in Western Civilisation, Chicago-London, 1986.
*Grégoire le Grand, Actes du colloque de Chantilly*, Centre culturel Les Fontaines, 15-19 septembre 1982, Paris, 1986, 690 p.
E. G. HINSON, *The Evangelization of the Roman Empire. Identity and Adaptability*, Macon, 1987, x-332 p.
G. STRAW, *Gregory the Great. Perfection in Imperfection*, Berkeley-Los Angeles-London, 1988, XIV-295 p.

## Chapter II

## DOCUMENTARY SOURCES

25. In these first ten centuries, the growth of national churches in various places led to collections of particular laws. Attempts were made to unify and reform canon law. We will treat, in turn, the writings of the first three centuries (to 313), those from the fourth to the ninth century (Nos. 34-85), and finally those from the ninth century to the Gregorian Reformation (Nos. 86-91).

26. For the first three centuries of Christianity, we may cite the Apostolic writings as the predominant source: the Acts of the Apostles and the letters of Paul give us occasional information on the attitude of the Christian communities and the qualities of the ministers of the Church (bishops, priests, and deacons).

In addition, the pseudo-apostolic writings contain disciplinary rules that arose and were accepted in one or more local Church communities. They are true legal norms of the post-Apostolic era, completely in the line of the law of the Apostles. As they are wrongly attributed to an Apostle, they are referred to as pseudo-apostolic writings. See W. PLÖCHL, *Geschichte des Kirchenrechts*, vol. I, Wien-München, 1960², p. 107.

27. The Greek *Didaché* or *Doctrina duodecim apostolorum* (the *Doctrine* or the *Teaching of the Lord by the twelve Apostles*) gives a series of prescriptions on baptism, fasting, the eucharist, the organization of the Christian community and its servants, the obligations of ministers and the faithful (e.g., in the Sunday liturgy), and the election and consecration of bishops, priests, and deacons. Most probably, it was drawn up toward the end of the first century by someone in the East, for a Christian community in Syria or Palestine.

The manuscript was unknown for centuries until Philotheus Bryennios, the Greek Orthodox metropolitan of Nicomedia, discovered a manuscript in 1875, in Constantinople, that dated from 1056. It came from the library of the patriarchs of Jerusalem. When Philotheus published it in 1883, it attracted a great deal of attention and has since often been translated and commented upon.

Edition

W. RORDORF-A. TUILLIER, *La doctrine des douze apôtres (Didaché). Introduction, texte, traduction, notes, appendice et index*, Paris, 1978 (= *Sources chrétiennes*, 248).

28. Around 218, Hippolytus of Rome († 235) wrote the *Traditio apostolica* for the Christian community in his city. He wrote in Greek, the language that was used by the educated clergy of Rome. Its content is very diverse and comprehensive. For example, it contains the oldest known ritual for the consecration of bishops, priests, and deacons, prescriptions for confessors, lectors, and catechumens, and regulations concerning baptism, fasting, the eucharist, church burials, church goods, and churches.

This is the only such work that originates in the West, but it did have a great influence on the collections from the East. Some say that it may not be considered among the pseudo-apostolic writings.

Editions

E. BOTTE, *La tradition apostolique de Saint Hippolyte. Essai de reconstruction*, in *Liturgiewissenschaftliche Quellen und Forschungen*, vol. 39 (1963), XLIV - 122 p.

E. BOTTE, *Hippolyte de Rome. La tradition apostolique d'après les anciennes versions. Introduction, traduction et notes*, Paris, 1984³ (= *Sources chrétiennes*, 11 bis), 152 p.

## Bibliography

A.G. MARTIMORT, "La tradition apostolique d'Hippolyte," *L'Année canonique* 23 (1979), pp. 159-173.
ID., "Nouvel examen de la 'Tradition apostolique' d'Hippolyte," *Bulletin de littérature ecclésiastique* 88 (1987), pp. 5-25.

29. After the *Traditio apostolica*, an anonymous author wrote the *Didascalia apostolorum*. This was around 230, when the Church had to defend itself against certain heresies (manicheism, gnosticism, pantheism, and so on). According to chapter 24, the work reports the discipline that the twelve Apostles applied a short time after their first council in Jerusalem (49). It mentions the obligations of bishops, priests, deacons, and deaconesses, prescriptions for fasting and the celebration of the eucharist and the relations with heretics and Jews, and advice for the Christian communities, married people, and widows. Because of its size and content, it is considered as the first attempt at a code of canon law.

## Editions

F.X. FUNK, *Didascalia et Constitutiones apostolorum*, 2 vols., Paderborn, 1905 (anastic reprint, Turin, 1964).
E. TIDNER, *Didascaliae apostolorum, canonum ecclesiasticorum, traditionis apostolicae versiones latinae*, Berlin, 1963.

30. The *canones ecclesiastici SS. Apostolorum* or *Constitutio apostolica ecclesiastica*, a collection of 30 chapters written in Greek, in Syria or Egypt, dates from around the year 300. The first fourteen chapters dealt with moral prescriptions, while the others dealt with the organization of the Church. Each Apostle has a turn in formulating a moral obligation or disciplinary measure.

31. The fifth pseudo-apostolic writing is the *Constitutiones apostolicae*, attributed to Clement of Rome (end of the first century). In reality, these eight books form a collection compiled in Syria or Palestine and dating from around 380.

It is a rewriting of the sources of the aforementioned pseudo-apostolic writings, and thus enjoyed great authority in the East.

In 691, the entire work, except for the eighty-five *canones apostolici*, was condemned by the Council of Trullo for errors that were particularly of a dogmatic nature.

Edition

M. METZGER, *Les constitutions apostoliques*, vol. I, Paris, 1985 (= *Sources chrétiennes*, 320); vol. II, Paris, 1986 (= ibid., 329); vol. III, Paris, 1987 (= ibid., 336).

32. The *Canones 85 apostolici* or *Canones apostolorum* were also attributed to the Apostles. It is assumed that they were written by the author or authors of the *Constitutiones apostolicae* in Syria toward the end of the fourth century, since forty-seven of the canons are found in the eighth book of the *Constitutiones apostolicae*. Thirty-seven or thirty-eight canons taken from the councils of the first four centuries were added. Later, they all circulated independently of the *Constitutiones*. Included in the *Synagogè* of Joannes Scholasticus, Patriarch of Constantinople (565-577), they were canonized by the Council of Trullo in 691. This gave them the force of law in the Eastern Church. They were also included in later Eastern collections. They treat the rights and duties of the clergy, ordinations, impediments to ordinations and irregularities, clerical crimes and punishments, the conditions of marriage and baptism, and attitudes towards heretics, schismatics, and Jews.

Dionysius Exiguus translated the first fifty canons into Latin in Rome in the beginning of the sixth century because they had been accepted by the popes, and he included them in his collection. This made them known in the West. The decree *De libris recipiendis et non*, an index of accepted and condemned books drawn up by an unknown author in Rome and placed under the patronage of Pope Gelasius, ranked the *canones 85 apostolici* among the apocrypha. This led Dionysius to remove them from his third edition. But the "damage" had been done: the *canones apostolici* were dispersed in the West and, in later years, several popes even declared them to be authentic. Several canons were taken up in later Western collections, such as the *Pseudo-Isidorianae,* the *Decretum Gratiani,* the *Compilationes antiquae,* the decretals of Gregory IX, and even the decrees of the Council of Trent.

33. In addition to these collections, which were generally from the East and all written in Greek, there are still other works from this period such as the *canones poenitentiales apostolorum,* the *constitutiones per Hippolytum,* and the *canones Hippolyti.* We will not treat them here because of their lesser importance or their inauthenticity.

However, it may not be forgotten that, in the first three centuries of Christianity, the writings of the Fathers and the ecclesiastical writers, the acts of the popes, and the acts of the councils, such as those of Carthage —where a council was held every year— the Council of Rome in 251, and the Council of Elvira in 300, are of importance for information on the ecclesiastical discipline of the time.

The norms were not technically well-formulated in "canons," since they were more akin to "customs" that had merely been written down. Nevertheless, there are traces of a juridical organization that manifests a special ordering in the Church.

Bibliography

A. VAN HOVE, *o.c.,* nrs. 117-130.
B. KURTSCHEID-F. WILCHES, *Historia iuris canonici,* vol. I, Rome, 1943, pp. 43-57.
A. STICKLER, *o.c.,* pp. 24-28.
W. PLÖCHL, *o.c.,* vol. I, pp. 105-111.
P. ANDRIEU-GUITRANCOURT, *o.c.,* pp. 605-610.
J. GAUDEMET, *Les sources du droit de l'Eglise en Occident du II$^e$ au VII$^e$ siècle,* Paris, 1985, pp. 15-28.

34. The second period runs from 313 through the Carolingian Restoration (ca. 850). We will describe the collections of canon law separately for two reasons. First, although the Church up to the time of Photius (end of the ninth century) remained unified, it was territorially divided into an Eastern and a Western Church, and secondly, the East exercised great influence on the West up to the ninth century because of its highly developed juridical works.

## A) In the East

### 35. Chronological collections

Beginning in the fourth century, canons, canonical letters, and imperial laws in ecclesiastical matters were compiled in chronological collections without any systematic or logical order. They are to be considered more as elements of legislation than as true legislation.

36. Between 342 and 381, an anonymous group compiled the *Syntagma canonum* or the *Corpus canonum orientale*. The collection consists of a few canons from the first Eastern councils, namely, Ancyra (314), Neo-Caesarea (between 314 and 319), Antioch (341), Gangres (343), and Laodicea (between 343 and 381). It was completed in Antioch under Bishop Meletios (thus also the name *Syntagma Antiochenum*). Twenty canons from the Council of Nicea were added to the beginning of the collection around 380, as were the canons of the First Council of Constantinople (381). This eastern collection was translated into Latin in the West during the fifth century (cf. below, no. 48).

The original eastern collection is known to us through a reference in the acts of the Council of Chalcedon (451) because the archdeacon of Constantinople read them. On the basis of this reference, attempts have been made to reconstruct them and, with the acts of Chalcedon itself, to compile all the legislation of that time. Since the idea was to make the collection as complete as possible, the canonical letters of the best known and most renowned bishops and Doctors of the Church were added, such as those of Athanasius (+373), Basil (+379), Gregory Nazianzen (+390), Gregory of Nyssa (+394), and Cyril of Alexandria (+414).

This *Corpus Orientale* can correctly be called the first documentary source of canon law. In his foreword to the *Codex Iuris Canonici* of 1917, Pietro Gasparri called it the *antiquarum collectionum fere omnium quasi principium et fons*.

37. In 692, the Synod of Constantinople took place. It was considered in the East as an ecumenical council that was intended

to fill in the gaps of the fifth (583) and the sixth (680-681) ecumenical councils (or, respectively, the second and third of Constantinople) as regards discipline. Hence, its name *Quinisextum*. It was also called the *collectio Trullana*, because the synod (*Concilium Trullanum*) met in the hall (Troullos) of the imperial palace.

The council approved, in the second canon, the revised and enlarged *syntagma canonum* or *antiochenum*. In the acts, 102 disciplinary measures were included in addition to the conciliar canons and positions of the Fathers. These disciplinary measures were already in force before they were included in the collection, which was promulgated later. The imperial laws of Justinian in ecclesiastical matters were added. Until the Photian Schism (867-879), this collection was considered to be the Code of the Eastern Church.

### 38. Systematic Collections

Law only becomes true law when it is grouped in a logical order or by subject.

The *Syntagma canonum* was continually expanded, which made it difficult to consult. The excess of laws led to many repetitions, while others were inappropriate for the time and place. This made their application difficult, incomprehensible, and even irresponsible.

The *Syntagma* is certainly not comparable to the Digests or the Code of Justinian. The need for systematization became increasingly critical, and a first attempt at systematic compilation was made in the sixth century. From then on, the papal decretals would also be mixed with the conciliar canons and merged into a whole.

### 39. The *Collectio 50 titulorum* was compiled around 550 by an Antiochene lawyer, Joannes Scholasticus, later patriarch of Constantinople (564-578). Following the example of the Pandects, which had just appeared, and perhaps at the request of Justinian himself, Joannes Scholasticus brought together under fifty titles the law of the Church that was then in use. In his foreword, he wrote:

«Ea quae passim ab ipsis definita sunt pro temporibus, in unum colligere magno studio enixi fuerimus, eaque in titulos quinquaginta distribuerimus, non ordinem quemdam et seriem numerorum servavimus....., sed similia similibus quantum fieri potuit copulantes et par pari capiti connectentes...», cfr G. VOELLUS — H. JUSTELLUS, *Bibliothecae iuris canonici veteris tomus secundus*, Paris, 1661, p. 500.

He obtained the contents principally from the *canones 85 apostolorum*, the *syntagma antiochenum* and the letters of St. Basil. In an appendix, he later added the civil constitutions relevant to ecclesiastical matters from the *Novellae* of Justinian. These last texts he grouped in eighty-seven chapters: the *collectio 87 capitulorum*. An abbreviated version, the *23 capitula ecclesiastica*, has also been ascribed to him.

40. At the end of the sixth century, an anonymous compiler brought together the *Collectio tripartita constitutionum ecclesiasticarum* consisting of the imperial laws in ecclesiastical matters from all the collections of Justinian and the commentaries in the *Novellae* of Athanasius Scholasticus. In the first half of the seventh century, four *novellae* of Emperor Heraclius (610-641) were added. The collection consists of three distinct parts (*tripartita*). The first part concerns the clergy, bishops, and religious (*personae*), the second deals with ecclesiastical matters and offices (*res*), and the third with the actions against heretics, Jews, and pagans (*actiones*). This work, the first complete collection of civil laws in ecclesiastical matters, met with considerable approval.

41. The systematic method was continued in what were called, in the eleventh century, *Collectiones nomocanonum*: collections of ecclesiastical (*canones*) and civil (*nomoi*) laws organized systematically or logically under one and the same title (*Staatlichrechtliche Materien in kirchlichen Angelegenheiten*, cf. W. Plöchl, *op. cit.*, vol. I, p. 275). In the other works, the civil laws were only added to the church laws in appendix.

At the end of the sixth century, an anonymous compiler put together the *Nomocanon 50 titulorum*, consisting primarily of the Church laws from the *Collectio 50 titulorum* and the civil laws of the *Collectio 87 capitulorum* of Joannes Scholasticus.

Around 629, the *Nomocanon 14 titulorum* was compiled, probably by the jurist Enantiophanes, from ecumenical and particular councils and from the *Syntagma Antiochenum* for Church laws and from the *Tripartita* and the *Novellae* of Heraclius for civil laws.

In addition to the collections of the Byzantine Church, there are those of other Eastern Churches: the Alexandrian, Antiochen, Armenian, Chaldean, and Melchite Churches. Indeed, each Church had its own law. All these collections give a picture of ecclesiastical legislation in the East up to Photius (857-886).

42. The acceptance and application of imperial law in the Church was necessary at the time because the Church itself did not promulgate universal law. Councils were held only on the occasion of unforeseen and transitory events in specific regions. Laws were only laws for specific occasions and had no universal character.

Justinian, in his *Codex* and *Novellae*, gave the law a more universal character. Many *Novellae* were already a partial synthesis and formed an ordered whole of themselves. Thus, *Novelle 123* (545) brought together in forty-four chapters everything that concerned the reception of orders, the qualifications of bishops, and the obligations of the clergy. The six chapters of the *Novelle 133* (539) gave detailed regulations regarding the monastic life.

Not only was the eastern imperial or civil law more universal and more abstract, the people of the East were of the opinion that the sovereign (the emperor) had received all power from God (*sacerdos et imperator*) over people, associations, and thus also over religious matters. The Church, therefore, accepted his law without question. Moreover, Justinian gave the impression that he was guided in his legislation by the old canons of the councils and by the writings of the Fathers. The difficulties of the Western Empire, to which the Pope had to give his full attention, and the minimal influence of the papal legates in the Eastern imperial court, encouraged the infiltration of civil law into canon law.

## B) In the West

43. After Photius (end of the ninth century), the Western and Eastern Churches went their own separate ways. The one Catholic Church with a more or less uniform law, although already territorially divided since Diocletian (284-305), definitively split with the Schism of 1054. The two churches developed their own law. The eastern Church continued in the line of Justinian without, however, exercising much influence on the western Church. The western Church developed its laws in the fashion of the East (i.e., first chronologically, then systematically), but it was two centuries behind the eastern Church.

44. Chronological collections

The earliest chronological collection we know of comes from Africa. It was in Latin and created rather spontaneously. In the fourth century, several synods were held in Carthage which gained renown throughout the Western world: "respectu activitatis conciliaris Ecclesia Africana inter alias eminet" (cf. A. Stickler, *op. cit.*, p. 34). At the beginning of each synod the conclusions of the previous synod were read and approved. Thus, cumulative chronological collections were formed which enjoyed great prestige, because of the approval. They found their way across their territorial borders and were very often included in other collections. They developed into "universal" law that greatly influenced the development and composition of the *ius commune*.

45. At the Third Council of Carthage in 397, the canons of the Council of Hippo of 393 were thus read and approved. The collection is know under the name of *Breviarium Hipponense* or *Breviatio concilii Hipponensis*. In 419, the Seventeenth Council of Carthage approved a compilation of about a hundred decisions of previous African councils (from 393 to 418) and added thirty-three new ones. Thus was formed the *Collectio Concilii Carthaginensis XVII*, which acquired great prestige not only in Africa but also in Europe (Spain, Gaul, and Italy) and even in the Eastern Church. Dionysius Exiguus gave it the name of *Statuta Concilii*

*Africani* and disseminated it by including it in his collection. Joannes Scholasticus translated the *Collectio Concilii Carthaginensis XVII* into Greek and, at the order of Justinian, included it in his *Synagogè*. We find the *Collectio* included in most later Eastern collections, such as the *Collectio Trullana*. Christophorus Justellus (1580-1649) edited the first Latin and Greek edition, and gave it the name of *Codex canonum Ecclesiae Africanae*, while, more correctly, it deserved only the title of *Registri ecclesiae Carthaginensis excerpta*.

The Council of Hippo in 427 marked the end of the golden age of African conciliar legislation. At a council held in Carthage in 525, the concern was more to call attention to the numerous canons of the African councils of the fourth and fifth centuries.

46. In Italy, the situation was very poor. While in the East, in Africa, and in Gaul, the many canon law texts were carefully collected, there seems to have been little concern in Italy for the development, preservation, and publication of Roman legislation. The causes of this were the religious and political situation of Italy at the time, the difficulties with Constantinople, and the rather weak personalities of the thirty-four popes from 498 to 701. In the few councils, only a small number of disciplinary measures were taken. Attention was focussed mainly on controversies about heretical movements. Only a few popes issued decretals, and these were of a local character. Among the most notable are Innocent I (401-417), Leo the Great (440-461), Gelasius (492-496), Symmachus (498-514), Hormisdas (514-523), Vigilius (537-555), Pelagius I (556-561), Gregory the Great (590-604), and Martin I (649-655).

There are two collections of papal decretals from before the pontificate of Leo I (440-461): the *Canones urbicani*, which appeared to be drafted in Gaul, and the *Epistolae decretales*, which probably originated in Rome. They consisted of decretals of the popes beginning with Innocent I (401-417) and are known to us only through Frankish collections from the middle of the sixth century (cf. below, no. 65).

During the papacy of Innocentius I (401-417), and most probably already during the reign of Julius I (337-352), a Latin collection of canons of the councils of Nicea (325) and Sardica (343/344) was available, known as the *Versio antiqua Romana* or *Vetus Romana*. We also know of the private collection, in Latin, of canons of the councils of the Eastern Church (Nicea, Ancyra, Neocaesarea, Gangres, Antiochia, Laodicea and Constantinople) and of the councils of Sardica and Carthago (419), which was in use in the first half of the fifth century. It probably had been put together in Rome between 419 and 450. Erroneously, it was called the *Versio Isidoriana seu Hispana*, since it had been found in the *Collectio Hispana* (mid seventh century) which includes the translations of the Eastern councils. It is this *Collectio Hispana* which is included in the "false decretals" of the ninth century. Some fifty years later, there appeared, in Rome (between 496 and 514), another collection, in Latin, of acts of the councils. They were called the *Prisca* by their publisher, Christorus Justel (1580-1649), who was very much impressed by the sentence of Dionysius Exiguus: "imperitiae *priscae translationem*." They are also called *Itala*, since they were mainly used in Italy.

The situation changed with Pope Gelasius I (492-496), who claimed full authority in religious matters. The Pope had to have the power to issue universal laws and to change the laws of his predecessors.

> «Ipsi Gelasio praecipuae partes tribuendae sunt, qui prae ceteris Pontificibus tum auctoritatem Ecclesiae in materiis religiosis, tum postestatem Romani Pontificis ferendi leges ecclesiasticas universales et decreta praedecessorum relaxandi», cf. A. VAN HOVE, *o.c.* p. 155.

This *Renascentia Gelasiana*, as Gabriel Le Bras and Alfons Van Hove call this period, although Jean Gaudemet has some reservations about this, continued up to Pope Hormisdas (514-523). From the acts of the councils — including those of the East — and the decretals of the popes, collections were made that comprised the universal law of the Church. In this unified law, the decretals of the popes gradually came to predominate. Cf. W.

Ullmann, *Gelasius I (492-496). Das Papsttum an der Wende der Spätantike zum Mittelalter,* in *Päpste und Papsttum,* vol. 18, Stuttgart, 1981.

47. In the chapter library of Freising there was a manuscript known as the *Collectio Frisigensis.* Because of its two separate volumes, the one containing the acts of the eastern councils and the other containing the decretals from Damasus I (366-384) to Gelasius I (492-496), it may be considered the first important mixed collection of canon law. It dates from just after 495 or from the very first years of the sixth century. According to some, it was certainly compiled in Italy and probably in Rome. According to Gaudemet, it is of Gallic origin.

48. The principal collection from this period, however, is the *Collectio Dionysiana,* named after its author, Dionysius Exiguus. This Scythian monk settled in Rome around 496, probably during the reign of Pope Anastasius II (496-498), the successor of Pope Gelasius. Shortly thereafter, he was appointed the head of the papal archives. He was the right man to bring together the scattered legislation and thus form a universal canon law.

At the request of two bishops, Dionysius translated the first fifty *canones apostolorum,* the canons of the Eastern Councils (cf. no. 36), and the *Collectio Concilii Carthaginensis XVII* of 419 into Latin. His work became the *Collectio-versio Dionysiana canonum conciliorum.* Dionysius edited another two versions. They were followed by a second collection of forty decretals of the popes of the fifth century, namely from Pope Siricius (384-399) to Anastasius II (496-498). This was the *Collectio decretalium Dionysiana,* which is the first collection consisting exclusively of papal decretals. Dionysius had found them in the older collections and in the archives of the papal chancellery. He published this work at the end of the pontificate of Pope Symmachus (498-514). The *Liber canonum* and the *Liber decretorum,* as both these collections were called, were considered by the author to be parts of a whole. As such they were called *Codex* or *Corpus canonum,* and later on *Collectio Dionysiana.* This collection was later supplemented with decretals from Innocent I to Gregory II (715-731), and with Roman councils up to 743. Thus, new forms of the *Dionysiana* resulted.

Dionysius excelled not only in his correct translations. He also accurately ordered the material and purified it of all that was dogmatic. The "Corpus" became a purely juridical work with exclusively disciplinary stipulations and with universal value. Therefore, he excluded from his third edition the *canones Apostolorum* and the canons of Sardes and of Africa, precisely because they were not accepted by the universal Church.

In the following centuries, the collection of Dionysius was very highly respected. In 774, Pope Adrian I sent it to Charlemagne as the official code of canon law for the Universal Roman Church. This collection was revised and supplemented, primarily with letters from Pope Gregory the Great (590-604), the only pope who created law in the sixth and seventh centuries. The intention was to reform the Frankish church after the model of the Roman tradition. In 802, the *Dionysio-Hadriana* was promulgated by the Synod of Aachen under the title *Codex Hadrianus*. In the Middle Ages, it became the *Liber canonum*. Its dissemination throughout Italy, France, Spain, Africa, and Ireland was without precedent.

Although the *Codex Hadrianus* is counted among the Italian collections, its existence was due to the knowledge and diligence of an Eastern monk. Actually, the intellectually poor capital of the old empire was incapable of such an accomplishment. The Eastern and African texts were not even known, nor, understandably, did anyone know the technique of collecting papal decretals. The Scythian monk was thus received with open arms in the western world and established his name there forever. In the Ancien Régime, the French Parliaments would refer to his work when they cited the old canons accepted in France in order to support their own positions. Claude Lepelletier, a minister of Louis XIV, preserved the writings for posterity by having them printed in 1687 on the presses of the Louvre.

49. In France, ecclesiastical centralization developed only under Charlemagne. Previously, there were no universally re-

cognized collections of canon law. Nevertheless, Gennadius, a priest of Marseille, compiled the *Statuta ecclesiae antiqua*, consisting of 105 canons, probably between 476 and 485 (cf. C. Munier, *Les Statuta ecclesiae antiqua*, Paris, 1960, 266 pp.). The author argued for the organization of provincial synods and for what we would today call diocesan priests' councils in order to control the exercise of power by the bishops. He devoted himself to the rehabilitation of the monastic spirituality of St. Basil, and focused the attention of the clergy on the benefits of asceticism, manual labor, and a simple life. The content of his work reflects a certain sensitivity to systematization.

Throughout the entire Middle Ages, this collection had considerable influence. The existence of many manuscripts and their citation in the Medieval canonical collections provide the best proof of this.

50. Pasquier Quesnel, an Oratorian (1634-1719), produced an edition at the end of the seventeenth century that he called the *Codex Canonum Ecclesiae Romanae*. This was the modern version of a private collection from Gaul or Italy from the end of the fifth century. His work has been called the *Collectio Quesnelliana*. This collection of ninety-eight canons followed precisely the trend of the Gelasian Renaissance. It contained canons from the first councils of the East and of Africa, decretals of eight popes, namely from Siricius to Gelasius I, letters from the French bishops to popes, and imperial constitutions against heretics. The random, mixed collection had a great influence in France until the time of the proclamation of the *collectio Dionysio-Hadriana* and the dissemination of the false decretals.

Many lesser known collections of the second half of the sixth century (e.g., *Coloniensis, Albigensis, Remensis, and Pithonensis*) also contained papal decretals alongside conciliar canons.

In the sixth and seventh centuries, more than fifty councils were held in Gaul and important disciplinary measures were taken. This resulted in new collections that contained the new regulations. This was in sharp contrast to what occurred in Africa and

Italy, where the legislative activity of councils and by decretals was never large enough to result in collections of new law. Noteworthy from the sixth century, for example, are the collections of Corbie, Lyons, Lorsch, and Albi; and from the seventh century, for example, those of Saint-Maur, Reims, Pithou, Bigot, Diessen, and Saint-Amand. The most outstanding, because of its quality and influence (cf. below, no. 56), is the *Vetus Gallica*, formerly called the *Collectio Andegavensis* (or "of Angers").

51. Spain was very well-organized politically and, in contrast to France, was ecclesiastically well-centralized around the See of Toledo. In addition to the annual councils, thirteen national meetings took place in this city from 589 to 702.

Thus developed the *Collectio Hispana chronologica*, better known under the ninth-century name of *Collectio Isidoriana* since it was attributed to Isidorus Hispalensis, Bishop of Toledo and author of numerous other works both spiritual and profane (cf. below, no. 92). The fact that the list (table) of the councils included in it ends with the Fourth Council of Toledo (633) also argues for his authorship. It was later supplemented with canons of later councils, particularly those of Toledo up to 694. At present, there is no agreement on the place, date, and authorship of the work. The object was certainly to compile as complete a collection of canonical norms as possible. Therefore, the *Hispana* gathered its material from sixty-seven councils, both eastern and western, which were placed in the first part. The second part contains 105 decretals from the popes from Damasus I (366-384) to Gregory the Great († 604).

By its inclusion in the false decretals, it became one of the major sources of many collections, and its fame extended across the borders of Spain to France, Italy, and Ireland. Thus, this collection, because of its scope and its renown, equaled that of Dionysius Exiguus. Alexander III (1159-1181) and Innocent III (1198-1216) recognized it as the *Corpus Canonum authenticum* for all of Spain.

Edition

G. MARTINEZ DIEZ, *La colleción canónica Hispana*, 4 vols., Madrid, 1966-1982.

## 52. Systematic Collections

In the West, of course, the chronological collections were also incomplete, difficult to consult, and sometimes even contradictory. Here, too, systematization and classification were the obvious solution.

53. In Africa, Fulgentius Ferrandus, deacon of the Church of Carthage, compiled the *Breviatio canonum* around 546. It is a practical compilation of the original canons that was intended for wide public use and consisted of 232 numbers classified under seven titles and drawn from the councils of the East and Africa (from 348 to 523). The African church used it until the twelfth century.

In the sixth or seventh century, a certain Cresconius wrote the *Concordia canonum*, a tractate on canon law. The first part concerns the consecration of bishops, monks, and priests, ecclesiastical discipline, heresy and other crimes; the second part deals with the sacraments, primarily penance and marriage, and the relationship between bishop and clergy. There is no agreement on the country of origin. The author is unknown, though some argue for Dionysius Exiguus. Indeed, the author used only the canons and decretals of the *Dionysiana*, which were now systematically ordered. The *Concordia* was used by many people for a long period of time.

Both collections bear witness to a well-organized ecclesiastical society on the African continent, which had been in contact with the Greek rather than with the French world. The influence of earlier Greek collections is clearly apparent.

54. In Italy, no one succeeded in producing any notable works. In Spain the *Capitula Martini* appeared shortly after 563, since the last canon mentioned is one of the First Council of Braga in 563. The well-ordered, clearly formulated codex of eighty-four

canons consists of two parts: the first deals with the bishops and the clergy, the second with the laity. The work was inspired primarily by the eastern councils. Inclusion in the *Hispana* enabled it to be widely distributed.

In the Middle Ages the *Capitula* was wrongly attributed to Pope Martin I (649-655). The term *papa*, however, can also refer to bishops, in this case the Archbishop Martin (520-580) of Braga in Portugal, a Hungarian by birth, who, as an eastern monk, came to Spain in 550 and founded the monastery of Dumio in the vicinity of Braga. In his work, he manifested a very civilized and fine humanitarian spirit.

55. On the basis of the *Hispana chronologica*, several systematic collections were compiled in the seventh century. The first of these was the *Excerpta*, which methodically groups 1633 canons into ten books divided into 227 titles. It was compiled between the Tenth (656) and the Eleventh (675) Councils of Toledo. On the basis of the *Excerpta*, an unknown author revised the *Collectio Hispana systematica* or the *Isidoriana systematica* between the Eleventh (675) and Twelfth (681) Councils of Toledo. At that time, 656 *tabulae* were drawn up, and an index on the basis of the titles of the canons was included.

The invasion of the Arabs in 711 put an end to legislative creativity in Spain until the Gregorian Reform.

56. In France, Luc d'Achéry († 1685), a Benedictine monk, published the work named after him, the *Dacheriana*. It is a fullfledged French methodical collection, which had been compiled in the beginning of the ninth century by an unknown secular priest, perhaps from Lyons, on the basis of the *Dionysio-Hadriana* and the *Hispana*. Its three books deal with penance, procedural law, and the law of persons. It was of great significance for the Carolingian reform and continued to exercise considerable influence until the Gregorian Reform.

Among the many chronological collections that were formed in Gaul (cf. above, no. 50), the methodically ordered *Vetus Gallica* is the most outstanding. It was most probably compiled in Lyons around 600 on the order of Bishop Etherius. Approximately four hundred canons were gathered together under sixty-four titles. It was intended to serve the internal reform of the Church and emphasized the predominant role of the metropolitans. It was widely known, as is witnessed by thirteen complete manuscripts and several fragments.

57. In the sixth and the seventh centuries, a number of councils were held in Britain (England, Ireland), which are relatively little known. Noteworthy are the Council of Hereford of 673 and the English councils of 691/692 and of 697, which promulgated several disciplinary canons.

Around 700, the first systematic collections were put together in Ireland (the conversion of the Irish Celts was completed only in the last quarter of the seventh century). Because of their special character, their influence was great. Thus, an unknown scholar collected in the *Collectio Hibernensis* not only canons of Irish synods but also, and this was an innovation, texts from Scripture and from the Latin and Greek Fathers. He confronted the canonical obligations with the commands of Christian morality, the primary source of all canon law. Thirty-four canons came from a synod held around 457 under the presidency of Saint Patrick.

## Editions

C. MUNIER - C. DE CLERQ, "Concilia Galliae (314-695)," *Corpus Christianorum: series latina*, vols. 148 and 148 A, Turnhout, 1963.

C. MUNIER, "Concilia Africae (345-525)," *Corpus Christianorum: series latina*, vol. 149, Turnhout, 1974.

H. MORDEK, *Kirchenrecht und Reform im Frankenreich. Die Collectio Vetus Gallica, die älteste systematische Kanonessammlung des Fränkischen Gallien. Studien und Edition*, (Beiträge zur geschichte und Quellenkunde des Mittelalters. 1), Berlin-New York, 1975.

J. GAUDEMET, *Conciles Gaulois du IV$^e$ siècle. Introduction, traduction et notes*, Paris, 1977 (= *Sources chrétiennes*, 241).

ID., *Traduttore, traditore. Les Capitula Martini*, in *Fälschungen im Mittelalter*. (Internationaler Kongress der Monumenta Germaniae Historica), München 1986, Vol. 2, Hannover, 1988, pp. 51-65.

## 58. Bibliography

A. VAN HOVE, *o.c.*, nos. 139-143, 145, 148-164.
A. STICKLER, *o.c.*, pp. 34-112.
W. PLÖCHL, *o.c.*, vol. I, pp. 273-286, 441-442.
P. ANDRIEU-GUITRANCOURT, *o.c.*, pp. 616-631.
J. GAUDEMET, *La formation du droit séculier et du droit de l'Église aux IV$^e$ et V$^e$ siècles*, Paris, 1979$^2$.
P. PINEDO, "Concordia canonum Cresconii," *Ius Canonicum* 4 (1964), pp. 35-64.
G. LIMOURIS, "Vie et œuvre de Denys le Petit," *Revue de droit canonique*, 37 (1987), pp. 127-142.

### C) Other Collections

59. In addition to chronological and systematic collections of canons of the Apostles and of the councils, of the decretals of the popes, and even of scriptural texts and writings of the Fathers, there are still other collections that influenced, to a greater or lesser degree, ecclesiastical society.

### 60. Collections of Civil Law

Collections of imperial or royal laws were often accepted, tacitly or explicitly, by the ecclesiastical authorities. Of course, these *leges in materia ecclesiastica* of the Roman and German emperors and the French kings, although these were not competent to legislate in ecclesiastical matters, certainly can be considered as sources of canon law.

61. Among the collections of Roman law, mention must be made of the *Codex Theodosianus*. It is the first authentic collection of the imperial constitutions in force, beginning with Constantine the Great. It was promulgated in 438 in the East and the West by order of, respectively, Theodosius II and Valentinian III. The first of the sixteen books contains two imperial constitutions on the episcopal courts; the sixteenth is devoted completely to ecclesiastical matters and contains 199 chronologically ordered prescriptions that deal with the clergy, churches, monks, heretics, Jews, and pagans.

62. The emperor Justinian (527-565) attached great importance to the ideal of unity in church, empire and legislation. The ancient empire would be reborn through military power and law, and clothed in a Christian garment. In order to achieve this, he compiled the imperial constitutions in twelve books, his *Codex Justiniani*, which he promulgated officially in 529. It is known to us only in the revised edition of 534. The first thirteen titles of the first book deal with the Church. In the other volumes, important prescriptions can be found, sporadically, on crimes, impediments to marriage, and divorce. Justinian's *Digesta* or *Pandectae* is a collection of texts from the great classical Roman jurists (Gaius, Modestinus, Papianus, Ulpianus, and Paulus). A commission of scholars and lawyers was assigned to make a convenient and practical compilation of the ancient law of the jurists. Repetitions and contradictions were to be eliminated, and obsolete and superfluous laws were to be discarded. A collection of fifty books resulted.

The four books of Justinian's *Institutiones* are a methodical, elementary handbook of Roman law, inspired by the *Institutes* of Gaius. The work dates from 533 and was intended especially for education in the law.

The *Novellae* were intended to fill out the Code. They contained the later constitutions of Justinian and his successors, Justin II (565-578) and Tiberius II (578-582), but they never became an official compilation. Their content is known to us only through references and citations in three private collections. Thirty-five of the 175 *novellae* concern the Church. This collection was later filled out with the *novellae* of various emperors up to Heraclius (+641) and was partially taken up into the *Ekloge Isaurica* of Leo III in 726.

In 1583, Dionysius Gothofredus combined the four Justinian collections and published them under the name of *Corpus iuris Civilis*, taking his lead from the collection published in 1500 of what was popularly called the *Corpus Iuris Canonici* in later years.

## Editions

Th. Mommsen-P. Meyer, *Theodosiani libri XVI cum constitutionibus Sirmondianis et leges novellae ad Theodosium pertinentes*, 2 vols. in 1, Berlin, 1905 (anastatic reprint, 1954, 1962 and 1970/71).

P. Krueger, *Codex Theodosianus*, Berlin, 1923-1926 (uncompleted: vols. I-VIII).

P. Krueger, Th. Mommsen, R. Schoell, G. Kroll, "Iustiniani Digesta, Iustiniani Institutiones, Codex Iustinianus, Novellae," *Corpus Iuris Civilis*, 3 vols., Berlin, 1862 (1872)-1895.

### 63. Bibliography

L. Wenger, *Die Quellen des Römischen Rechts*, Vienna, 1953.
J. Gaudemet, *Institutions de l'antiquité*, Paris, 1982².
W. Kaser, *Römische Rechtsgeschichte*, Göttingen, 1967².
H. F. Jolowicz - B. Nicholas, *Historical Introduction to the Study of Roman Law*, Cambridge, 1972³.
P. Frezza, *Corso di storia del diritto romano*, Rome, 1974³.
J. E. Spruit, *Enchiridion. Overzicht van de geschiedenis van het Romeins privaat recht*, Deventer, 1977².
W. Kunkel, *Römische Rechtsgeschichte*, Cologne-Vienna, 1980⁹.
V. Arangio Ruiz, *Storia del diritto romano*, Naples, 1978⁷.
A. Söllner, *Einführung in die Römische Rechtsgeschichte*, Munich, 1985³.
A. Guarino, *Storia del diritto romano*, Naples, 1981⁶.
R. Derine, *Schets van het Romeins privaatrecht. Uitwendige en inwendige geschiedenis*, Antwerp, 1982, pp. 21-114.

64. In the eighth and ninth centuries, in Northern Italy, extracts were selected from the collections listed above, for the use of the clergy. The *Excerpta Bobbiensia*, containing eighty-six chapters, treated of such things as the hierarchical order, monks, and ecclesiastical goods; the *Lex Romana canonice compta* has 371 chapters.

With the "barbarian" invasions of the Western Roman Empire, another culture competed with Roman culture. The Visigoths and the Burgundians (East Gaul) permitted the Romans to maintain their Roman law, albeit with modifications. Thus, the former Roman subjects lived under the old Roman law while the "barbarians" had their own law, of which almost no texts have survived. Some of the Roman collections have been preserved. One example is the *Lex Romana Wisigothorum* (so called in the nineteenth century), an "anthology" primarily of the imperial laws of the three codices, *Gregorianus, Hermogenianus,* and *Theodosianus,* and the *Novellae posttheodosianae,* the *sententiae Pauli,* the *Institutiones Gaii,* and so on. It was promulgated in Toulouse in 506 by Alaric II, King of the Visigoths (485-507) and was therefore called, in the sixteenth century, the *Breviarium Alaricianum.*

Edition

M. CONRAT, (COHN), *Breviarium Alaricianum. Römisches Recht im Fränkischen Reich in systhematischer Darstellung,* Leipzig, 1903 (anastatic reprint, Aalen, 1963).

A similar collection, the *Lex Romana Burgundionum,* was promulgated around 500 by Gundobad, King of Burgundy (474-516). With the downfall of the Burgundian kingdom in 534, it was superseded by Germanic law.

In the western part of the Frankish kingdom (West Gaul), Roman law remained in force as the personal law of the Gallo-Roman population. With the Roman urban population, the Church also lived under Roman law (*Ecclesia vivit lege romana*).

65. Up until the sixth century, most of the episcopal sees of Gaul and Germania were still occupied by bishops of Roman origin. Only at the end of the seventh century would the integration of Romans, Gallo-Romans, and Germans be complete. Most of the names of the bishops from then on are of German origin. Parallel with this, the power of the Frankish kings grew steadily. Hence, most of the collections of Frankish law *in materia ecclesiastica* were made in the ninth century. The royal prescriptions soon became the only source of law.

In the Merovingian period, these royal prescriptions were called decrees, edicts, or constitutions. In the Carolingian period, they were called *capitula.* So, the Merovingian and Carolingian collections of royal prescriptions came to be called the *capitularia.* The *capitula* dealt not only with purely civil law but also with ecclesiastical matters. These *capitula* were drawn up with the aid of the bishops, who generally belonged to the royal aristocracy.

The *capitularia* of Ansegisus, Abbot of Fontenelle (†834), contained prescriptions of Charlemagne (768-814) and Louis the Pious (814-840), grouped in four books of which the first two dealt with ecclesiastical matters and the last two with civil matters. The collection was written in 827 and ratified two years later by Louis the Pious. The *capitularia* of Benedictus Levita (middle of the ninth century) form a sequel to it.

66. For the list of *capitularia*, cf. A. Tardif, *op. cit.*, pp. 269-272; P. Andrieu-Guitrancourt, *op. cit.*, pp. 655-656; F.L. GANSHOF, *Recherches sur les capitulaires*, Paris, 1958.

67. *Libri paenitentiales* or *paenitentialia*

Among the ancient Romans, a penalty always involved public penance. The first Christians adopted this practice, but this was unknown to the "barbarians," for whom punishment consisted of *Wehrgeld*, a private monetary fine, the amount of which was determined from a pre-established list in function of the nature of the crime committed. The private penalty compensated for the suffering that was incurred by the crime. The Church quickly adapted to this new usage and introduced a similar system for its members, including the use of fines. Partially under the influence of monastic practice, particularly on the British Isles, where private confession was obligatory for the monks, public penance gradually disappeared.

Beginning in the sixth century, all kinds of *paenitentialia* appeared in the West. They contained lists of very specific penances to be imposed by the confessor for specific sins confessed in private. Generally, they are private works written by individual authors. *Canones paenitentiales* were known earlier [Councils of Elvira (ca. 300), Ancyra (314), Nicea (325)], but never before had these "penalties" been compiled in such collections.

68. On the British Isles, such *paenitentialia* appeared very early, generally under the influence of Irish monks.

Columban (543-615), a monk from Bangor, became the spiritual father of the *Liber de paenitentiarum mensura taxanda*. This work was compiled around 573 in the monasteries of Luxeuil in France or Bobbio in Italy, which he had founded himself.

Cummeanus Fota or Longius (592-662), the Abbot-Bishop of Clonfert in Scotland (not, as used to be thought, the Abbot of Hy or Iona), wrote the *Iudicia Cummeani*.

The *Discipulus Umbrensium*, which is also of British origin, was erroneously attributed to Theodorus († 690), Archbishop of Canterbury, and was therefore called *Iudicia Theodori Cantuariensis*.

The *paenitentiale* of the Venerable Bede († 735), an Anglo-Saxon monk from the Abbey of Jarrow and Doctor of the Church, was also well known on the continent. Some bishops even required that their priests always have this book with them, together with the forty homilies of Saint Gregory and the martyrology. Egbert († 766), Archbishop of York, probably compiled such a *paenitentiale*, too, but it did not enjoy the same renown.

69. On the continent, these lists were generally called *Iudicia Canonica*. They were very numerous between 750 and 825, particularly in Germany, Gaul, and Italy. These included the *paenitentiale* of Halitgar, bishop of Cambray (817-831); the two *paenitentiale* of Hrabanus Maurus, archbishop of Mainz, a ninth century compilation out of the *Dionysio-Hadriana* and *Hispana*; and the eleventh century *paenitentiale* of Fulbertus Carnutensis of Chartres. This multiplication of the number of *paenitentialia* and the differences in penance created a need for unification. Gradually, the "summaries" also disappeared. They were considered "useful suggestions" rather than fixed, unchangeable taxes. In any case, they were considered outmoded and could no longer be imposed in practice. Increasingly, the fines were replaced by prayers and indulgences. One was obliged to give alms and to fast or to go on a pilgrimage. Furthermore, the significance of fines declined even more with the revision of sacramental theology in the thirteenth century, which reflected the idea that penance itself was not an essential element of confession.

70. After the middle of the seventeenth century, the *Libri paenitentiales* were again studied because they contain a treasury of information not only on customs, usages, and mores or the development of the cult in the West, but also on the law regarding marriage and divorce, and even on medicine and hygiene. Thus, it is not surprising that works were written like *Die Bussordnungen der Abendländischen Kirche* by H. Wasserschleben (Halle, 1851; anastatic reprint, Graz, 1958), *Die Bussbücher und die Bussdisziplin der Kirche* (Mainz, 1883) and *Die Bussbücher und das kanonische Bussverfahren* (Düsseldorf, 1898) by J. Schmitz (both anastatic reprints, Graz, 1958). These are still the basic studies on the *paenitentialia*.

71. Bibliography

A. Van Hove, *o.c.*, nos. 273-276, 287-292.
A. Stickler, *o.c.*, pp. 89-92, 104-106, 112-113.
W. M. Plöchl, *o.c.*, vol. I, pp. 442-443.
P. Andrieu-Guitrancourt, *o.c.*, pp. 643-650.
L. Bieler, "The Irish Penitentials," *Scriptores latini Hiberniae*, vol. 5, Dublin, 1963.
P. Ciprotti, *Penitenziali anteriori al secolo VII*, Camerino-Milan, 1966.
C. Vogel, *Les « Libri paenitentiales »* (*Typologie des sources du moyen-age occidental*, fasc. 27), Turnhout, 1978 (completed A. J. Frantzen, 1985).
M. G. Muzzarelli, *Una componente della mentalità occidentale: i Penitenziali nell'alto medio evo* (*Il mondo medievale*, no. 9), Bologna, 1980.
R. Kottje, *Die Bussbücher Halitgars von Cambrai und des Hrabanus Maurus. Ihre Überlieferung und ihre Quellen* (*Beiträge zur Geschichte und Quellenkunde des Mittelalters*, vol. 8), Berlin-New York, 1980, xix-297 p.
A. J. Frantzen, *The Literature of Penance in Anglo-Saxon England*, New Brunswick, 1983.
G. Hägele, *Das Paenitentiale Vallicellianum I. Ein oberitalienischer Zweig der frühmittelalterlichen kontinentalen Bussbücher. Uberlieferung, Verbreitung und Quellen,* Sigmaringen, 1984, 107 p.
P.J. Payer, *Sex and the Penitentials. The Development of a Sexual Code 550-1150*, Toronto, 1984.
F. Kerff, *Das sogennante Paenitentiale Fulberti. Ueberlieferung Verfasserfrage, Edition*, in *Zeitschrift der Savigny-Stiftung für Rechtsgeschichte. Kanonistische Abteilung* 73 (1987), pp. 1-40.

## 72. Liturgical Books

As a community, the Church is organized by disciplinary measures. Its reason for existence, which can be found in Holy Scripture, with the Apostles, and in the pseudo-apostolic writings, is the public worship of God, which should be organized according to certain rules. It is for the bishops to issue these rules. In the West, this led to the creation of prayer and song books. The *sacramentarium* is a prayer book from which the priest or bishop could recite or sing during Mass. Often it included prayer formulas for the administration of other sacraments, except for extreme unction, and of sacramentals such as the consecration of churches and bells, and burials, because these were closely related to the celebration of the eucharist.

The *Sacramentarium Veronense*, called the *Leonianum*, was compiled in the beginning of the seventh century and erroneously attributed to Pope Leo the Great (440-461). Neither is the *Sacramentarium Gelasianum* of the same period to be attributed to Pope Gelasius I (492-496). In 595, Pope Gregory the Great (590-604) officially proclaimed a liturgy that was written down in the course of the seventh century in the *Sacramentarium Gregorianum*. Additions were made around 788 by Pope Adrian and sent to Charlemagne as the *Sacramentarium Gregorio-Hadrianum*.

The present *Lectionarium* which consists of the *Epistolarium* and the *Evangeliarium*, was created from the *Liber comicus* or *Comes*, which contained the Scriptural texts that were read by the deacon, subdeacon, or lector.

The *Antiphonare* or *Graduale* contained the antiphones and the responses that had to be sung by the choir.

The *Ordo* or *Caeremoniale* contained the rituals or "rubrics" that were to be fulfilled during Mass. Such books existed by the end of the sixth century. From them developed the *Rituale Romanum* (1614) and the *Caeremoniale episcoporum* (1600). The latter was intended for more solemn ceremonies that were celebrated in cathedrals and collegial churches by bishops (cf. below, no. 214).

Because the Mass was also celebrated privately from the beginning of the Middle Ages and because it was difficult to buy all these books separately, missals were produced. The oldest missal we know of is that of Bobbio from the seventh century.

In order to administer the sacraments and the sacramentals, there were small manuals: *agenda, liber agendorum, pastorale, rituale, manuale* and so on. The bishop could find in the *Pontificale* the same directions for the sacraments and sacramentals that had to be administered by him. These manuals appeared by the ninth century. Noteworthy is the *Pontificale Romano-Germanicum* of about 950, written by a monk from Mainz. Using this model, Guillielmus Durantis produced, in 1292, his famous *Pontificale*, which was accepted and published by Rome in 1495. It became the principal source for the *Pontificale Romanum* that Clement VIII promulgated for the universal Church in 1595.

Finally, the breviary is the thirteenth-century compilation of *psalteria, antiphonaria, passionaria, homiliaria, martyrologia, kalendaria, collectaria* or *orationaria*, and *hymnaria* that were used in the choral office.

### 73. Bibliography

A. VAN HOVE, *o.c.*, nos. 182-184.
A. STICKLER, *o.c.*, pp. 416-422.
P. ANDRIEU-GUITRANCOURT, *o.c.*, pp. 657-660.
J. DESHUSSES, *Le sacramentaire Grégorien. Ses principales formes d'après les plus anciens manuscrits. Edition comparative*, 3 vols., Freiburg, 1971, 1979, 1982 (*Spicilegium Friburgense*, nrs. 16, 24, 28).
A. CHAVASSE, "Le sacramentaire, dit Léonien, conservé par le Veronensis LXXXV (80)," *Sacris erudiri* 27 (1984), pp. 151-190.
*Medieval Liturgy. An Introduction to the Sources*, Washington, 1986. (revision and translation by W. G. STOREY - N. K. RASMUSSEN of C. VOGEL, *Introduction aux sources de l'histoire du culte chrétien au moyen âge*, Spoleto, 1981).

### 74. Collections of Formulas

On the basis of models or *formulae*, public or private juridical acts could be drawn up. They are a useful source for becoming acquainted with the content of the existing law and the administrative jurisprudence.

At the request of Leander, Bishop of Paris, the monk Marculf, in around 660, compiled the private *formulare* in two books.

Between 685 and 742, the *Liber diurnus Romanorum Pontificum* was produced. It is a collection of ninety-nine universal formulas of the acts from Honorius I (625-638) to Adrian I (772-795). Later, four appendices containing thirty-one formulas were added. The papal chancellery used it until the pontificate of Gregory VII (1071-1085). Included in it are the election of the Pope, the appointment of bishops, the granting of the pallium and of privileges, and the establishment of benefices. Yves of Chartres and Gratian found in it a rich source of documentation to confirm their collections.

75. Bibliography

A. Van Hove, *o.c.*, nos. 247-248.
A. Stickler, *o.c.*, pp. 66-67; 440-441.
W. M. Plöchl, *o.c.*, vol. I, pp. 450-451.
P. Andrieu-Guitrancourt, *o.c.*, pp. 656.
T. Von Sickel, *Liber diurnus Romanorum Pontificum*, Vienna, 1889 (anastatic reprint, Aalen, 1966).
L. Santifaller (reprint H. Zimmermann), *Liber Diurnus* (*Päpste und Papsttum*, X), Stuttgart, 1976.
H.H. Anton, "Der Liber Diurnus in Angeblichen und verfälschten Papstprivilegien des früheren Mittelalters," *Fälschungen im Mittelalter. Internationaler Kongress der Monumenta Germaniae Historica, München, 1986*, vol. 3, Hannover, 1988, pp. 115-142.

76. *Capitula episcoporum* or *Statuta dioecesana*

Episcopal decrees, some proclaimed in a diocesan synod, attempted to apply decisions of provincial councils or general church laws to the local church by means of supplementation, adaptation, and development of practical rules.

Their content varies from church dogma, discipline, and mores to liturgy and ritual. They are also interesting from the point of view of economics, geography, and philology.

Examples of well-known statutes are those of Theodulfus, Bishop of Orléans (end of the eighth century) and of Hincmar, Bishop of Reims (852, 858, and 874). Because of their great value, Gratian included several of them in his decree.

77. Bibliography

A. VAN HOVE, *o.c.,* no. 176.
A. STICKLER, *o.c.,* pp. 114-116.
P. ANDRIEU-GUITRANCOURT, *o.c.,* pp. 641-642.
O. PONTAL, *Les statuts synodaux* (*Typologie des sources du moyen âge occidental,* fasc. 11), Turnhout, 1975.
P. BROMMER, "Die bischöfliche Gesetzgebung Theodulfs von Orléans," *Zeitschrift der Savigny-Stiftung für Rechtsgeschichte. Kanonistische Abteilung* 60 (1974), pp. 1-120; ID., *Die Rezeption des bischöflichen Kapitularien Theodulfs von Orléans,* in *ibid.,* 61 (1975), pp. 113-160.
J. GAUDEMET, "Les statuts épiscopaux de la première décade du IX$^e$ siècle," *Proceedings of the Fourth International COngress of Medieval Canon Law, Toronto 1972,* (*Monumenta Iuris Canonici,* series C: *subsidia,* vol. 5).
P. BROMMER, «*Capitula episcoporum*». *Die bischöflichen Kapitularien des 9. und 10. Jahrhunderts* (*Typologie des sources du moyen âge occidental,* fasc. 43), Turnhout, 1985.

78. Collections of "False" Documents

Not only were the pseudo-apostolic writings apocryphal, but as Innocent I (401-417) complained in 414, there was an abundance of false letters. Initially, they remained individual documents, but after 850 whole collections were put together. The "forgeries" were made to free the Church from secular power. The ecclesiastical patrimony had to be secured from the hands of the secular owners, for ecclesiastical property had to serve a spiritual end. The clergy had to refrain from all activities (hunting, politics) that conflicted with their vocation. By the institution of the privilege of jurisdiction, bishops, priests, and religious could only be judged by ecclesiastical courts. The recovery of the eclesiastical disciplinary law also enhanced the prestige of the clergy. Celibacy, as well as a reappreciation of marriage, which was considered by many to be a magic or pagan rite, emphasized the salvific task of the priest. In order to achieve this, the clergy emphasized the superiority of the Pope and of the entire eccleciastical hierarchy. This authority had to form a unity against secular power. Appeal was made not only to authentic works (the bible, patristic writings, civil and canonical stipulations) but also to falsifications. In general, it is assumed that the "forgeries in service of the Church" of the ninth century are to be attributed to groups of intellectuals, probably monks, who used famous names as pseudonyms.

79. The *Hispana* of Autun (*Augustodunensis*) is considered to be the first attempt at pseudo-Isidorian forgery. It is based on the *Hispana chronologica*, and introduces a better ordering in the texts and adds apocryphal material.

80. Little is known about the *capitularia Angilramni*. Undoubtedly, they are from the hand of an author who, like Benedict Levita (cf. no. 82), wanted to break the secular power over the Church. They were named after Angilramne, abbot of Sens and later bishop of Metz (769-791) and court chaplain of Charlemagne. Indeed, it was thought that they were either written by Angilramne, who presented them to Pope Adrian in 785, or that they were given by this pope to Angilramne. Therefore, the collection is also called *Capitula Hadriana, Codex Hadrianus*, or *Synodus Romana*. It consists of seventy-one chapters of varying sizes.

81. Benedict, a deacon (*levita*) of the Church of Mainz, set out around 850 to fight the interference and the abuses of the secular power *ad liberandam ecclesiam a potestate saecularium*. Three-fourths of his *Capitularia* are apocryphal. They contain texts he composed himself alongside modified texts from the Holy Scripture, the works of the Fathers, and authentic collections.

82. The *Collectio pseudo-Isidoriana* or the *Decretales pseudo-Isidorianae* begins with the words "*Incipit praefatio S. Isidori*" such that, up to the fifteenth century, people were convinced that it was from the hand of Isidore of Seville or *Hispalensis* († 636). How-

ever, it seems to have been written between 847 and 852 by one or more authors from the Frankish Kingdom (Reims or Le Mans) or possibly by a group of clerics attached to the royal court chapel of Charles the Bald. The Collection consists of three volumes and contains the fifty *Canones apostolorum*, about ninety papal letters or decretals from the year 90 A.D. (St. Clement) to 731 (Gregory II), almost all forgeries, and generally distorted canons of the councils from 325 (Nicea) to 683 (the Thirteenth Council of Toledo). The authors used the *Hispana Augustodunensis* as their basis. Their intention was completely in the line of the previous collections, that was, to confirm and reorganize papal supremacy and to protect a united Church consisting of a multiplicity of particular churches gathered around Rome against secularization and excessive civil interference.

In the twelfth century, parts of the collection were included in the canonical collections. Thus, the collection acquired authority in Rome and throughout the Catholic world. Its apocryphal character was recognized only in the fifteenth century although, already in the twelfth century, there were doubts expressed by Petrus Commestor, Gothofridus Viterbiensis, and Stephanus Tornacensis among others about the authenticity of some of the decretals. From then on, they are referred to as false decretals or *Pseudo-Isidoriana*, although authentic decretals and conciliar canons also appear in them.

Edition

P. HINSCHIUS, *Decretales Pseudo-Isidorianae et capitula Angilramni*, Leipzig, 1863 (anastatic reprint, Aalen, 1963).

## 83. Bibliography

A. VAN HOVE, *o.c.*, nos. 293-305.
A. STICKLER, *o.c.*, pp. 117-142.
W.M. PLÖCHL, *o.c.*, vol. I, pp. 445-449.
P. ANDRIEU-GUITRANCOURT, *o.c.*, pp. 661-677.
S. WILLIAMS, *Codices Pseudo-Isidoriani*, (*Monumenta iuris canonici*, series C: *subsidia*, vol. 3), New York, 1971.

A. MARCHETTO, *Episcopato e primato pontificio nelle decretali pseudo isidoriane. Ricerca storico-giuridica*, Rome, 1971, XLVII - 312 p.

H. FUHRMANN, *Einfluss und Verbreitung der pseudo-Isidorischen Fälschungen. Von ihrem Auftauchen bis in die neuere Zeit* (Schriften der monumenta Germaniae historica, 24, I, II, III) 3 vols., Stuttgart, 1972-1974.

P. LANDAU, *Gefälschtes Recht in den Rechtssammlungen bis Gratian*, in *Fälschungen im Mittelalter. Internationaler Kongress der Monumenta Germaniae Historica. München 1986*, vol. 2, Hannover, 1988, pp. 11-49.

84. Bibliography of the Second Period (nos. 34-82)

A. VAN HOVE, "De bronnen van het kerkelijk recht tot het begin der zesde eeuw," *Mededelingen van de koninklijke Vlaamse Academie voor wetenschappen, letteren en schone kunsten van België*, 1941.

J. GAUDEMET, *L'Église dans l'Empire Romain (4ᵉ et 5ᵉ siècles)*, Paris, 1958.

A. FAIVRE, *Naissance d'une hiérarchie. Les premières étapes du cursus clérical* (Théologie historique, XL), Paris, 1977, pp. 207-422.

J. GAUDEMET, *La formation du droit séculier et du droit de l'Église aux IVᵉ et Vᵉ siècles*, Paris, 1979², pp. 143-176.

J. GAUDEMET, *Les sources de droit de l'Église en Occident du IIᵉ au VIIᵉ siècle*, Paris, 1985, pp. 33-161.

C. MUNIER, *Vie conciliaire et collections canoniques en Occident, IVᵉ-XIIᵉ siècles*, Paris, 1987.

85. The third period, from the ninth century to Gregory VII (1073-1085), is undoubtedly the most important for the formation of canon law. Numerous local works of a specific nature were created. Scriptural and patristic texts, conciliar canons and papal decretals, civil laws, and penitentials were arranged systematically. This led directly to the systematization and diffusion of the useful prescriptions. It cleared the way for Gregory VII's ecclesiastical reform.

86. In Italy, the *Collectio Anselmo dedicata*, by an anonymous, probably Italian, cleric, belongs among these works. Of purely Roman inspiration, it was written around 882 and dedicated to Anselm II, Archbishop of Milan (882-897). It consists of

twelve books, the first of which is a tractate on the primacy of the Pope. There is also the *Collectio canonum in V libris*, compiled by a Benedictine monk of Farfa between 1014 and 1023. It deals with the reform as envisaged by Henry II (1002-1024) and Benedict VIII (1012-1024).

Edition

M. FORNASARI, "Collectio canonum in V libris," *Corpus Christianorum, continuatio medievalis*, part. VI, 2 vols. (vol. 1, I-III, 1970).

87. For France, the canonical collection of Abbon, abbot of the Benedictine Abbey of Fleury († 1004), one of the most learned and influential persons of his time, is of particular importance. It was compiled between 988 and 996 and consists of chapters on law and church history. It describes the rights and duties of the civil authority toward the Church, the rights and duties of the monasteries in both civil and canon law, and also the relationship between bishops and monasteries. The power of jurisdiction of the bishop contrasted with the exception of the monasteries and their immunities and privileges. Indeed, the reform of the monastic system was inseparably bound up with this exemption. In the second part of the collection the monastic state is treated.

88. Even more renowned were the German collections. At the end of the ninth century, the Carolingian Renaissance "par les vices des hommes et les malheurs des temps" (cf. F. Cimetier, *op. cit.*, p. 43), had reached its zenith. Rathbod, the Archbishop of Trier, wanted to learn about the religious situation in his diocese, and therefore appointed synodal witnesses, both priests and laity, to inform him of crimes and scandals. To Regino of Prüm, Abbot of Prüm († 915), who was in exile in Trier, he gave the task of compiling a manual for these *testes synodales*. Regino finished his two-volume work, the *Libri duo de synodalibus causis et disciplinis ecclesiasticis*, around 906. One volume considered the clergy, the other the laity. Regino included, in addition of lists of questions, sanctions for the crimes committed and even formulas for

excommunication and absolution. It soon became a handy *vademecum* for the bishop conducting visitations.

Edition

H. WASSERSCHLEBEN, *Reginonis abbatis Prumiensis libri duo de synodalibus causis et disciplinis ecclesiasticis*, Leipzig, 1840, 554 p. (anastatic reprint, Graz, 1964).

89. Between 1008 and 1022, Burchard, Bishop of Worms († 1025), collected his *Decretum*, which was intended to inform the clergy about canon law. He worked on a definitive edition until his death. He tried to reform the Church by increasing the power of the bishops, although he did not reject the primacy of the Bishop of Rome. He fought strongly against simony, and he recommended that the clergy live in communities with celibacy as the rule. In contrast to Abbon of Fleury, he emphasized the subordination of the monasteries to the bishop and made no reference to their exemption or other privileges. The emancipation of the Church from civil authority was an ever recurring theme.

The twenty books of the *Decretum* consist of the *Collectio Anselmo dedicta*, the *Libri de synodalibus causis*, the *Collectio Dionysio-Hadriana*, and the *Pseudo-Isidorianae*. The nineteenth book, *Corrector et medicus*, was a penitential dealing with confession and was used until the fifteenth century. Burchard made it a practical handbook for teaching the young clergy, for synods, and for visitation journeys. It had an immense influence.

Bibliography

M. KERNER, *Studien zum Dekret des Bischofs Burchard von Worms*, 2 vols., Aachen, 1969.
H. MORDEK, "Systematische Kanonessammlungen vor Gratian: Forschungsstand und neue Aufgaben," *Proceedings of the Sixth International Congress of Medieval Canon Law, Berkeley 1980*, Città del Vaticano, 1985, pp. 185-201 (Monumenta Iuris Canonici, series C: *subsidia*, Vol. 7).
G. PICASSO - G. PIANA - G. MOTTA, *A panee acqua. Peccati e penitenze nel Mediaevo. Il Penitenziale di Burcardo di Worms*, Novara, 1986.

90. Bibliography (third period, nrs. 85-89)

A. VAN HOVE, *o.c.*, nos. 306-307, 312-313, 315, 318-319, 321-322, 335.
P. FOURNIER - G. LE BRAS, *Histoire des collections canoniques en Occident depuis les Fausses Décrétales jusqu'au Décret de Gratien*, 2 vols., Paris, 1931-1932 (anastatic reprint, Aalen, 1972).
A. STICKLER, *o.c.*, pp. 144-148.
W.M. PLÖCHL, *o.c.*, vol. I, pp. 449-451; vol. II, pp. 462-465.
P. ANDRIEU-GUITRANCOURT, *o.c.*, pp. 678-728.
G. FRANSEN, *Les collections canoniques* (*Typologie des sources du Moyen-Age occidental*, 1973, no. 10), Turnhout, 55 p., pp. 12-16, 25-27 (completed edition, 1985).
*Nouvelle histoire de l'Église*, vol. II, *Le moyen âge*, Paris, 1969, pp. 141-156, 167-175, 199-222.

Chapter III

THE SCIENCE OF LAW

91. In the first centuries of Christianity, up to the time of Charlemagne, canon law was only treated in passing in works on dogma or morality. The "obligation in conscience" was far more important than a concise, abstract rule: "ab aliis scientiis sacris non erat distincta, ... opera exclusive canonica nulla, quamquam multa canonica reperiuntur in scriptis S. Patrum ac scriptorum ecclesiasticorum, quae postea in collectiones iuris canonici sunt inserta," cf. A. Van Hove, *op. cit.*, no. 402. Nevertheless, in this period we find the first traces of a "science" of canon law.

92. Isidore of Seville or Hispalensis (560-636) had the reputation of being the most learned man of his time. This Archbishop of Toledo (599/600-636) was proclaimed *Doctor Ecclesiae* in 1722. He wrote nineteen works in all. His *Etymologiarum sive Originum libri XX* in twenty volumes can be called an encyclopedia of contemporary human knowledge. Isidore dealt with the most divergent matters. Volume V, *De legibus et temporibus*, was taken up almost in its entirety in the *Decretum Gratiani*. It is volume 82 of J.P. Migne's *Patrologia Latina*, cols. 9-728.

93. The systematic collections were an early attempt to produce works on the science of law. For France, we know of the *Statuta ecclesiae antiqua* (476-485) and the *Collectio Andegavensis* (ca. 600).

The *Capitula Martini* (ca. 563) came from Spain; Africa had the *Breviatio canonum Ferrandi* (ca. 546) and the *Concordia Cresconii* (seventh century). The *Collectio Hibernensis* (ca. 700) led the way in Ireland. The *Libri paenitentiales*, at least insofar as they were compiled in a systematic way, can be considered scientific tracts.

94. During the reign of Charlemagne (750-900) and immediately thereafter, priests and bishops had to be sufficiently informed about canon law, according to express requirements of the king and the Pope. Pope Celestinus I in 429 and the Fourth Countil of Toledo in 633 had already stipulated this, and the *Capitularia Caroli Magni* and the *Capitula episcoporum* stressed the same thing.

The systematic collections of this period, the *Dacheriana* (France, ca. 800) and the *Hispana systematica* (Spain, between 675 and 681) can be considered the first forms of a science of law.

Also worth mentioning are the works of Rabanus Maurus (ca. 780-856), the Abbot of Fulda and, in 847, Archbishop of Mainz: *De institutione clericorum libri III* from 819, and its shorter version, *De sacris ordinibus, sacramentis divinis et vestimentis sacerdotalibus*, both treaties on priestly duties. They had a considerable influence and a broad impact until the twelfth century. Many of the manuscripts date from the second half of the eleventh century and the beginning of the twelfth century, the period of the Gregorian reformation.

Both Hincmar, Archbishop of Reims (806/845-882), who was praised for his exceptional knowledge of Roman law, and Abbon of Fleury published scientific writings. Cf. J. Devisse, *Hincmar, archevêque de Reims (845-882)*, vol. III; *Appendices, Bibliographie et index*, Geneva, 1976, pp. 1395-1465; K. SCHIEFFER, "Hincmar von Reims," *Theologische Realenzyklopädie*, vol. 15, Berlin-New York, 1986, pp. 355-360.

95. From 900 to the end of the eleventh century, the theological-canonical works dealt predominantly with specific subjects. Peter Damian of Ravenna (1007-1072), hermit from Fonte Avellana (ca. 1035), consultor to various popes and Cardinal Bishop of Ostia (1057), explained his opinion on the degrees of consanguinity in his book *De parentelae gradibus* of 1063. He opposed the concept of the Ravenna School by saying that the degrees of consanguinity in marriage law had to be reckoned not according to the method of Roman law but according to canon law.

Tithes, sacrileges, and immunities were also commonly treated subjects.

Study

R. KOTTJE, H. ZIMMERMANN (ed.), *Hrabanus Maurus. Lehrer, Abt und Bischof*, Wiesbaden, 1982, IX-208 p.

Edition

W.M. STEVENS, "Rabani mogontiacensis episcopi de computu," *Corpus Christianorum. Continuatio mediaevalis*, vol. 44, Turnhout, 1979, pp. 163-331.

J. RYAN, *Saint Peter Damiani and his canonical Sources. A Preliminary Study in the Antecedents of the Gregorian Reform (Pontifical Institute of Mediaeval Studies. Studies and Texts, 2)*, Toronto, 1956, XVIII-213 p.

C.M. LAWSON, *Sancti Isidori episcopi Hispalensis de ecclesiasticis officiis (Corpus Christianorum*, ser. Lat., 113.), Turnhout, 1989, 163 en 160 p.

## 96. Bibliography

A. VAN HOVE, *o.c.*, nos. 402-408.
B. KURTSCHEID - F. WILCHES, *o.c.*, vol. I, pp. 215-230.
W.M. PLÖCHL, *o.c.*, vol. I, pp. 455-457.

SECOND PERIOD

# FROM THE GREGORIAN REFORM TO THE COUNCIL OF TRENT
(Second half of the eleventh century to 1545)

### Chapter I

### HISTORICAL CONTEXT

97. The years from 1000 to 1300 were of particular creative significance for Europe. Western Europe emerged for the first time as the most dynamic region of the world: several national states arose, international trade and industry flourished, religious organization and the expansion of Christian culture reached an unprecedented high point.

The twelfth and the thirteenth centuries are rightly seen as *la sintesi medievale, l'éveil de l'Europe, un temps de plénitude et d'apogée, Lumière du Moyen Age, les vrais Grands Siècles de notre histoire, die Blüte des Mittelalters*.

A) Centralization of Papal Power

98. The Christian religion was a vital force in medieval Europe. It had an enormous effect on the daily life of ordinary people. Religious enthusiasm was reflected in the crusades (1095-1453) and in the approval of new religious orders (eleventh to the thirteenth century).

These two factors led to strong support for the centralization of papal power, which is perhaps the most important characteristic of the Late Middle Ages. By means of an internal reform of the Church, several popes tried to build Western Europe into a solid Christian community based on religious ideals and subjected to Christian morality, which transcended royal or imperial law.

After the fall of the Western Roman Empire (476), the Church slowly but surely grew out of its ancient Mediterranean setting and bound itself to the nations of the developing West. The final break with Constantinople in 1054 meant a definitive rupture with its Greek and Eastern origins. In the feudal Western Europe of the Early Middle Ages, the Church found shelter with local large landowners. Under the feudal system of these first centuries, the landowners felt themselves obliged to provide for the religious development of their subjects. Often the lord would build a church within the walls of his domain and oblige his serfs to convert to Christianity. As lord and owner of the church with its domain, he collected tithes and even appointed the parish priest. The church and everything that pertained to it became the family property of the local lord, benefiting in full from his power and thereby acquiring the eloquent name of *Eigenkirche* or proprietary church. This patriarchal organization caused the bishops to lose virtually all their power over the rural parishes. Even entire abbeys with their vast lands and income came into the hands of the laity. The Church was largely secularized.

99. The further development of the Church from the tenth century onwards proceeded along a totally different line in the western part of Western Europe.

After feudal rights became hereditary in the ninth century, western France consisted of quasi-independent states. The local lords acted more and more independently of their feudal lord, the French king. Only after the twelfth century was he gradually able to expand his power again.

The system of proprietary churches continued in Western France up to the eleventh century. From around the year 1000, the population began to expand rapidly, and the domanial system proved inadequate. The so-called *villes neuves*, rural settlements with municipal rights, were soon established in undeveloped regions. The rise of the new religious orders, which functioned independently of the lord, and the revival of trade after 1050 contributed to the dissolution of the domanial system. The Church gradually took over the countryside through the parishes.

The power of the bishops — and of the Pope — slowly but surely expanded while the influence of the local lords waned.

In Eastern France, the reforms of Emperor Otto gave an entirely new turn to ecclesiastical policy. The Frankish kings had already introduced feudalism in the eighth century. Otto I, the Great, (912/936-973) adopted lay investiture with the introduction of the so-called Ottonian system whereby administrative powers were given to ecclesiastical functionaries. Because the clergy could have no legitimate offspring, the offices could not become hereditary and always reverted to the king. Otto I succeeded in appointing abbots and bishops and then gave them administrative powers. Thus arose the German Imperial Church. The prince-bishops and the abbots had full ducal rights in their areas: they could collect tolls and mint coins, exercise ecclesiastical as well as civil jurisdiction, and had the right to raise armies. The price that the Church paid for this was high. Not only did the emperor of the Holy German Roman Empire (crowned by the Pope from 2 February 962 onwards) appoint the ecclesiastical dignitaries in his territory, he also educated them at his court. Moreover, by the *privilegium Ottonianum* of 962, he acquired the oath of loyalty and, in 963, the right of veto in papal elections. All of this was given in exchange for protection of the papal states.

100. Among the monks, and particularly those of the Benedictine community of Cluny, opposition arose against the generally lax attitude of the Church toward its functionaries. Sacraments, sacramentals, ecclesiastical benefices, dignities, and jurisdiction ought no longer be commercialized, and simony ought to be abolished. The control of the state over ecclesiastical appointments and property had to cease, and bishops and abbots were no longer to engage in worldly pleasures (hunting), politics, and war, since Nicolaitanism was considered one of the most important causes of the evil.

Pope Leo IX (1048-1054) had already tried to reinforce his power over the clergy in order to eliminate abuses among them and limit the interference of the laity in ecclesiastical matters.

Later popes challenged these irregularities under the slogan of *libertas ecclesiae*. So, for example, Nicholas II withdrew the papal elections from the Italian noble families by 1059. Henceforth, the Pope was to be chosen by the cardinal-bishops. With Gregory VII (1073-1085), the investiture struggle reached its zenith. Cf. U.R. BLUMENTHAL, "Gregor VII," *Theologische Realenzyklopädie*, vol. 14, Berlin-New York, 1985, pp. 145-152; I.S. ROBINSON, "Pope Gregor VII (1073-1085)," *The Journal of Ecclesiastical History* 36 (1985), pp. 439-483; J. CHOUX, "Grégoire VII," *Dictionnaire d'histoire et de géographie ecclésiastiques*, vol. 36, 1987, col. 1424-1433. In the twenty-seven theses of his *Dictatus Papae* of 1075, he established the political-ecclesiastical program for future popes. Recent scholarship is not at all positive about the so-called Gregorian reform and its effects. Cf. J. GAUDEMET, "Regards sur l'histoire du droit canonique antérieurement au Décret de Gratien," *Studia et documenta historiae et iuris* 51 (1985), pp. 80-82, 105-106.

When, in 1071 and 1075, the German Emperor Henry IV (1056-1106) exercised his right to appoint bishops in spite of the papal prohibition and set the imperial bishops against the Pope at the Diet of Worms in 1076, Gregory VII promptly excommunicated him. In order to regain the favor of his Christian subjects, the Emperor walked barefoot to Canossa in the winter of 1076-1077. In 1122, the conflict was temporarily settled by the Concordat of Worms: the Pope accorded a certain voice to the lay rulers in the appointment of the higher clergy, but he always retained the final word. In 1179, Alexander III ruled that henceforth a Pope could be elected only by a two-thirds majority of the cardinals.

With Pope Innocent III, the theocracy reached a high point in its external aspects, cf. W. Inkamp, *Das Kirchenbild Innocenz' III (1198-1216) (Päpste und Papsttum)* vol. 22, Stuttgart, 1983; G. SCHWAIGER, "Innocenz III," in *Theologische Realenzyklopädie*, vol. 16, Berlin-New York, 1987, pp. 175-182. The pope was the independent leader of the Church, and supreme over the spiritual and the temporal princes. The Holy See had absolute power over all other spiritual and secular power. In the words of the pope in 1204:

«Pontificem, quem in beato Petro sibi vicarium ordinavit, super gentes et regna constituit, evellendi, destruendi, disperdendi, dissipendi, et aedificandi, et plantandi ei conferens potestatem» (*Patr. Lat.*, CCXV, 277; *Bullarium Romanum*, III, 107).

A clear illustration of this was the conflict between Innocent III and King Philippe-Auguste of France, which was ultimately decided in favor of the Pope.[1]

101. Internally, this theocracy was expressed in the exercise of power by the Pope over the entire universal Latin Church. In 1302, Aegidius Romanus (Egidio Colonna) wrote in his *De ecclesiastica potestate*: "Summus pontifex, qui tenet apicem ecclesiae et qui potest dici ecclesia, est timendus et sua mandata sunt observanda, quia potestas eius spiritualis, celestes et divina, et est sine pondere, numero et mensura" (lib. III, cap. ult., in fine, cf. R. SCHOLTZ, *Aegidius Romanus. De ecclesiastica potestate*, Weimar, 1929, 209 p. (anastatic reprint, Aalen, 1961).

By means of decretals, the Pope exercised supreme legislative power in the Church. He had compilations of laws made and gave them the force of law for the entire Church. Many popes in the twelfth and the thirteenth century were great jurists: Alexander III (1159-1181), Innocent III (1198-1216), Gregory IX (1227-1241), Innocent IV (1243-1254), and Boniface VIII (1294-1303).

The Pope also represented the highest administrative power: he acquired increasing influence on the appointment of bishops and on the local diocesan organization. More and more, legates with special missions were employed. From the twelfth century onward, the Pope had the exclusive right of canonization, and he approved religious orders and universities.

Finally, the Pope also considered himself the supreme judicial power. In every sector, the Pope had the power to take a case to

---

[1] Cfr C. VAN DE WIEL, *La légitimation par rescrit el l'évolution de la «sanatio in radice» chez les décrétalistes jusqu'en 1650. Étude historico-juridique*, in *Revue de droit canonique*, 9 (1959) pp. 39-66; ID., *De wettiging door rescript en de evolutie van de sanatio in radice bij de dekretalisten tot 1650. Historisch-juridische studie*, in *Tijdschrift voor Rechtsgeschiedenis* 27 (1959), pp. 290-312.

himself. He acted as the umpire of the Christian West. The external development of power was linked to an internal restructuring of the Church: the establishment of administrative services (consistories, Roman curia) by means of centralization, bureaucracy, and well-organized tax collections.

B) New Ways to Perfection

102. The Revival of the Ancient benedictine Order

Benedict of Nursia (ca. 480 - ca. 547) had been a hermit in Subiaco, a village east of Rome. His way of life soon attracted followers among the youth of his time, whom he gathered into a religious community, first in Subiaco and then in Monte Cassino (529), and to whom he gave advice and rules. These were inspired by, among other things, the *regula magistri* and the rules in force among the Egyptian desert monks.

After the end of the sixth century, the Rule of St. Benedict spread throughout all of Italy, the rest of Europe, and the British Isles, becoming the general law for all monks. Benedict is rightly called the patriarch of the monks in the West. His followers, although very modest by nature, formed, individually and collectively, a permanent part of society. Their influence extended to every sector — spiritual, liturgical, artistic, economic, and even administrative — and they made an enduring mark on all of Western Christianity.

In addition to their life of prayer, the monks devoted themselves to education, caring for the sick and elderly, and sheltering travellers and pilgrims. They even exercised some jurisdiction. In the sixth and seventh centuries, communities were created in many places that accepted the Rule of St. Benedict, such as Saint Remigius at Reims (550), Saint Peter at Luxeuil (590), San Colombano at Bobbio (612), Saint Ouen at Rouen (645), Saint Benedict of Fleury at Saint Bènedict on the Loire (648), Saint Remacle at Stavelot (650), Saints Peter and Paul at Malmédy (650), Saint Waudrille at Fontenelle (649), Saint Peter at Lobbes (654), Saint Trudo at Sint-Truiden (660), and Saint Peter and Saint Bavo at Ghent (ca. 660-670). Later, others like Cornelimünster near Aachen (815) and Mont-Saint-Michel (960) were founded. Thus, there is no better name than "Benedictine" or "monastic era" for the period of Western church history between the death of Saint Benedict and the death of Saint Bernard in 1154.

103. The invasions of the Normans, Saracens, and Hungarians made an end of the Carolingian Empire. Secularism and a general decline of religious life were the inevitable consequences. Many newly founded abbeys were abolished.

From the tenth century on, this decline of religious life was stopped by the foundation of the Abbey of Cluny (910), by the Abbot Berno of Chaume and William of Aquitaine. Since the dependence of the monasteries on the secular and the spiritual lords had been one of the major causes of the ecclesiastical decline in the ninth century, they guaranteed their monastery freedom in its own affairs. Independence from the jurisdiction of the diocesan bishop was stipulated in the act of foundation and later ratified by papal privileges (exemption). The monasteries came directly under papal authority and lived according to the rule of St. Benedict: discipline and asceticism, choral prayer and renewed piety, attention to the liturgy and obedience to the abbot of the mother house, Cluny.

Under Abbot Odilo (994-1048), the 'congregation' of Cluny developed. Many abbeys joined and implemented the reform in the surrounding regions. Abbot Odilo maintained authority over the abbeys and the priories he founded himself. Abbot Hugo (1049-1109) continued the work of his predecessor in the same line. Notwithstanding their intense prayer life, the monks remained open to the world. They practiced science, were not averse to politics, and maintained good contacts with emperors and kings.

Cluny reached its highpoint at the end of the eleventh century. The reform at this point counted 1450 communities, all of which came under the Abbot of Cluny. Cluny itself had grown from a community of fifty members to one of seven hundred. It was the center of the spiritual and moral reform of the West. The monastic buildings were of high architectural quality, and the church was the largest in Christendom. In addition to the monastic and ecclesiastical reform movement, which led to a deepening of the Christian life, Cluny, by its influence, also demonstrated the importance of religion in the life of society. Indirectly, Cluny also exercised a strong influence on history by calling attention to the place of the Church and the Pope in the world, to the current abuses in the Church (e.g., simony) and to the great task that the Church had taken upon itself.

Without exaggeration, one may say that, in this period, the Abbot of Cluny was the *de facto* leader of Western Europe. Cluny could glory not only in spiritual but also in secular power. The Cluniac reform was carried out in the spirit of the pseudo-Isidorian decretals with the support of the German princes, such as Otto I (936-973) and Henry III (1039-1056).

Nevertheless, Cluny was not free of the influence of the feudalization of the West. Although it is true that the abbot never delegated his power and had no representative, he himself carried out tasks for the Emperor in addition to handling ecclesiastical matters. Cluny strove to preserve independence, to maintain its autonomous authority over its priories, and to safeguard itself completely from imperial and episcopal jurisdiction. Its direct dependence on the Holy See (exemption) meant a very valuable support for the Pope. By the end of the eleventh century, Cluny had representatives in the highest ecclesiastical circles and prepared the way for the ecclesiastical and political reforms of Gregory VII.

Benedictine monasticism was long the only accepted form of monastic life. It did undergo cycles, however. The entire later period of Benedictine history was marked by alternating periods of prosperity and decline. Indefatigable zeal gave rise to new centers, while laxness in administration and observance of the rule led to the disappearance of other, once flourishing abbeys. Reactions in the form of reforms constantly recurred. The most important one is that of 1132 by Peter the Venerable (1122-1156).

P. Schmitz, *Histoire de l'Ordre de Saint-Benoît*, 7 vols., Maredsous, 1948-1956.
*Benedicti regula*, 2 ed. by R. Hanslik, Vienna, 1977 (*Corpus scriptorum ecclesiasticorum latinorum*, vol. 75).
H. Rochais - E. Manning, *Règle de Saint-Benoît*, Rochefort, 1980.
J.F. Tschudy - F. Renner, *Der heilige Benedikt und das benediktinische Mönchtum*, St. Ottilien, 1979.
B. Kominiak, *Loci ubi Deus quaeritur. Die Benediktiner Abteien*, St. Ottilien, 1980.
Art. "Benedikt von Nursia, Benediktiner, Benediktusregel," *Theologische Realenzyklopädie*, vol. 14, 1985, pp. 538-560, 573-577.
M. Pacaut, *L'ordre de Cluny (909-1789)*, Paris, 1986.

104. Successive reforms led to the formation of several orders throughout Europe.

From the second half of the tenth century onwards, other monks lived a much more stringent life, such as the eremitical life of the desert fathers, and were inspired by the Rule of St. Benedict. Moreover, they did not approve of the worldly concerns of the feudal abbots, who often acted as advisors to kings. Monks should not occupy themselves with the management of large estates and the collection of rents, tithes, taxes, and interest. Therefore, a group of hermits who wanted to devote themselves totally to prayer formed in Northern Italy.

105. Saint Romualdus (951-1027), as abbot of the Cluniac abbey of Saint Appolinaris in Classe near Ravenna, could not reconcile himself with the slackness within the monastic walls. He withdrew to the swamps around Ravenna to live the austere life of a hermit.

In Fonte Avellana near Pesaro, he founded a community to which Peter Damian (1007-1072) belonged. Peter Damian wrote Romualdus' biography, gave the community its rules, and led it to prosper. In 1057/58, he became a cardinal and leader of the Roman reform movement. Around 1023/24, Romualdus had built in the isolated area of Camaldoli, east of Florence, five individual cells and a place of prayer. From this grew the Camaldolese order, which was approved in 1072 by Alexander II. The monks devoted themselves primarily to the study of canon law. Because of their strongly eremitical life, they could only gather in the chapter room and the church.

106. Around 1039, in Vallombrosa near Florence, Joannes Gualbertus († 1073), a monk of Saint Miniato in Florence, founded the Vallombrosiani. His monks accepted the strict enclosure and vowed eternal silence. Their way of life was thus closer to eremitical than to cenobitical (*Koinos* = communal) monasticism. At present, they exist only in Italy.

107. Bruno of Cologne (1030/35-1101), the last prefect of the cathedral school of Reims, withdrew with six companions in 1084 to the isolation of the wild, rocky valley of the Chartreuse near Grenoble. The foundation was named after the place, and the religious were given the derived name of Chartreusians. Their way of life still strongly resembled that of the Camaldolese. The monks came together only three times a day in the church for the eucharist and choral prayer. They had no common areas except for the church, the chapter room, hall, and the refectory, and they lived separately in small houses constructed around an atrium. Only on feast days did they eat together, but even then in complete silence. They ate no meat and also vowed almost perpetual silence. They spent their days in prayer, labor in the fields, or copying manuscripts. They were assisted by *conversi*, lay brothers, who lived in separate buildings. Because of their austerity, the Chartreusians escaped the laxness that marked the later Middle Ages. They still remain a small elite among the religious orders of the Church, the only medieval order that has never needed a reform: *Cartusia numquam reformata, quia numquam deformata* (Innocent XI).

M. ZADNIKAR - A. WIENAND (eds.), *Die Kartäuser. Der Orden der Schweigenden Mönche*, Cologne, 1983.

G. POSADA, *Der Heilige Bruno, Vater der Kartäuser. Ein Sohn der Stadt Köln*, Cologne, 1987.

J. HOGG, "Kartäuser," *Theologische Realenzyklopädie*, vol. 17, Berlin-New York, 1988, pp. 666-673.

108. The monastic structures of Cluny clung too tightly to the feudal type, so a high degree of secularization threatened many Benedictine abbeys. Internal tensions about monastic ideals ultimately led to the foundation of Cîteaux.

Twenty-one monks of the Benedictine abbey of Molesmes desired to live a more secluded and austere life. They settled in 1098 under the leadership of Robert, Abbot of Molesmes (†1111), at Cîteaux (*Cistercium*) in a wild and isolated region south of Dijon. Abbot Robert returned to his abbey, but the austere Cistercian order continued.

The Cistercians rediscovered the ideal of Benedict as reflected in his rule, which was no longer being applied by the Cluniac monks in its pure form.

In 1119, Pope Callixtus II ratified the constitution *Charta Caritatis*, the rule that had been drawn up in 1113-1119 by Stephanus Harding, the second abbot (1109-1133) of Cîteaux. It formed a sharp reproach to the wealth and the less austere way of life of the Cluniac monasteries. The monks refused to own land, churches, and feudal incomes. The ideal was a return to a life of poverty in austere monasteries. By reducing and simplifying the common prayers and the liturgical solemnities, the monks created a time vacuum that, mindful of the *Rule* of St. Benedict, they filled with manual labor and spiritual reading.

109. In 1115, Saint Bernard (1090/91-1153), a monk of Cîteaux, founded Clairvaux (*Clara Vallis*) with twelve other monks. Under his leadership, the order expanded greatly: by the time he died, there were 343 Cistercian abbeys, of which he himself had founded sixty-six. In 1300, there were about 690 abbeys, and, around 1500, approximately seven hundred monasteries for men and nine hundred for women. A good three hundred and fifty sermons and five fundred letters from him have been preserved.

The Cistercians settled in the most isolated regions. In contrast to the Cluniac abbey and its priories, the foundations were autonomous communities, abbeys *sui iuris*, and the order did not want to be exempted. It had its constitutions approved by the local bishop before making a foundation. Although they promoted the economic life, they refused all income that did not derive from their own labor. Cîteaux exercised no special power over them. All the abbots formed a collegial authority, and all the monks lived in complete solidarity with the chapter of abbots of Cîteaux, on which each abbey was represented by its abbot.

Because of the influence of Cîteaux as a center of authority and because of the strictly uniform observance of the rule, a close bond existed between the abbeys. This new formula was the secret of the success of the Cistercian Order.

The Cistercians greatly influenced the revival of Christianity. Their monasteries, built with extreme austerity, were true centers of culture, and are world renowned up to our day. The old foundations have vitually all disappeared.

L.J. LEKAI, *The Cistercians. Ideals and Reality*, Kent, 1977.

J.B. VAN DAMME, "Moines-Chanoines-Cîteaux. Influences réciproques," *Aureavallis. Mélanges historiques réunis à l'occasion du neuvième centenaire de l'abbaye d'Orval*, Liège, 1975, pp. 15-54.

E. MIKKERS, "Robert de Molesmes et l'ordre de Cîteaux," *Dictionnaire de Spiritualité*, vol. 13, 1988, col. 736-814.

110. Another kind of community was founded by Norbert of Gennep, a former canon of Xanten (1082-1134). In Prémontré near Laon, he gathered men and women who devoted themselves to evangelical life. They lived in great austerity and earned their living by craft labor and agriculture. Gradually, their communal live was structured according to the observations of the *ordo novus*. For their internal structure, they honored the principle of the independence of the associated houses. Prémontré became the model monastery, where the abbots of the Norbertine abbeys met regularly in general chapter to watch over fidelity to the postulated monastic ideal. In 1126, Norbert was appointed Archbishop of Magdeburg and there, too, he installed his *canonici*. From the outset, his followers adopted the rule of Saint Augustine. They gave themselves to the service of the Church by sanctifying themselves and by caring for the salvation of their fellows. Therefore, they served in parishes that had previously been proprietary churches. The Norbertines or Premonstratensians expanded considerably, to the point that there were more than a hundred abbeys throughout Western and Central Europe by 1156.

W.M. GRAUWEN, *Norbertus aartsbisschop van Maagdenburg (1126-1134)*. (Verhandelingen van de Koninklijke Academie voor Wetenschappen, Letteren en Schone Kunsten, Klasse der Letteren, XL, 86), Brussels, 1978, LXII-690 p.

E. PETIT, *Norbert et l'origine des Prémontrés*, Paris, 1981, 327 p.

111. Women, too, took part in the Gregorian Reform. In addition to the Benedictine and Cistercian nuns, there were Beguines, who lived a community life in a beguinage, which was an enclosed area close to a city. Every beguinage had its own church, its own priests, and chaplains. They were under the authority of one to four superiors, depending on the number of beguines. Beguines who did not have sufficient income to have a separate residence lived in one of the convents, in which, for a small compensation, they were given food and lodging. Most of their expenses were covered by income from property with which the founder had endowed the community. The community was administered by a superior or a mistress. The beguines did manual labor, taught girls, cared for the sick, and buried the small fee, they were given food and lodging. Most of their expenses were covered by income from property with which the founder had endowed the community. The community was administered by a superior or a mistress. The beguines did manual labor, taught girls, cared for the sick, and buried the dead. They never had a general rule or took vows and thus were not *religious* in the strict sense. They were members of a free, local association. There were only local statutes, which often differed from community to community. This disturbed the Church authorities, and all the more so as some beguines were falling into heresy. The Council of Vienne condemned and suppressed the movement in 1311, but John XXII permitted its revival in 1350.

112. Soldiers for Pope and Church: The Military Orders.

In the Middle Ages, it was not only the monastic vocation which was very popular. The chivalric ideal also appealed to many young men. In the military orders, these two ideals were joined. Moreover, the crusades in this period needed soldiers who were motivated by religious zeal. Many defenders of the true faith went to Jerusalem to liberate the Holy Land from the Moslems, who had captured it in 1071. After the city was recaptured in 1099, the foundation of the Christian Kingdom of Jerusalem brought a mass of pilgrims to the holy places.

The military orders were founded to take care of these pilgrims during and after their long, dangerous, and arduous journey. In their rule, in addition to the three ordinary religious vows, they also vowed hospitality, safety, and medical care for the pilgrims.

The Hospitallers or the Order of the Hospital of Saint John of Jerusalem was originally a fraternity that was founded in 1099 to operate the Hospital of St. John in Jerusalem. Its members took care of both healthy and sick travellers on their journey to and from the East. In 1120, they were changed into a military order, an elite corps that accompanied the armies on their crusades. In 1291, the headquarters was transferred to Cyprus, in 1309 to Rhodes, and finally in 1530 to Malta, from which came the name of Maltesians.

113. Eight French knights founded the Templars or the Knights of the Temple in 1119 to accompany and protect pilgrims on their journey to Palestine. Baldwin II, King of Jerusalem, gave them quarters in his palace, which was built on the site of the Temple of Solomon, from which they took their name. The order was suppressed by Clement V in 1312 at the Council of Vienne.

A. LEMEYRE, *Guide de la France Templière*, Poitiers, 1975.

These two orders rapidly expanded throughout all of Europe. But they remained overwhelmingly Latin and primarily French oriented. They had the three vows and lived according to the monastic rule of Saint Augustine. The German or Teutonic military order, founded in 1190, was also a hospital fraternity that was changed in 1198 to a military order. This order contributed to the Christianization of Prussia and remained strongly German oriented.

H. BROOCKMANN, *Die Deutsche Orden*, Munich, 1981.

114. The Mendicant Orders and the Contemplatives.

Around 1200, the zeal of the Gregorian Reform in Europe gradually disappeared. Wealth and love of ease did not at all encourage strict discipline. Heresies (Albigensians, Waldensians, and the Cathars) made ready inroads into the middle classes. The spiritual needs of the new cities were great. Unexpectedly, in this crisis situation, the mendicant orders arose and converted the thirteenth century into a new era of apostolic and pastoral zeal and of intellectual life.

115. In 1215, St. Dominic (ca. 1170-1221) gathered around him in Toulouse his "Dominicans", which Honorius III approved at the end of 1216. Dominic charged them with preaching the Catholic faith and morals in order to fight the heretics. Training priests to be preachers was something new, since preaching belonged only to the episcopal office. Dominic brought his followers together in monasteries that became true houses of theological study. The young Dominicans were educated and the older ones received additional training. Dominic combined cenobitism with an apostolic nomadism. In imitation of the apostles, he sent his members out to beg and preach. This was unique for the time. The order, initially intended as a preaching order for the Diocese of Toulouse, expanded throughout Europe under the name of *Ordo Praedicatorum*, as Dominic proposed to the Pope. From the beginning, the order founded centers for study in Paris, Oxford, Cologne, Montpellier, Bologna, and elsewhere.

In contrast to the autocratic practice of Cluny, the Dominican cloisters were administered by a superior, who was elected for a fixed term and assisted by a chapter. Each province had a provincial, and a provincial chapter was chosen each year. The provincial chapters elected a life-time general and a general chapter for a fixed term.

In Prouille in Southern France, Dominic founded a monastery for women in 1206, which developed into his second order.

M.H. VICAIRE, *Dominique et ses Prêcheurs*, Fribourg-Paris, 1979[2].
ID., *Histoire de Saint Dominique*, 2 vols. Paris, 1982[3].

116. St. Francis of Assisi (1181/82-1226) emphasized living in total poverty and brotherly love. Innocent III approved his style of life orally in 1210 and gave him and his followers permission to preach. Francis made up a rule for his Friars Minor (*fratres minores*), which, after revision, was ratified in 1223 by Honorius III. By the end of the thirteenth century, the Franciscan order had more than 30,000 members in two hundred monasteries. Disputes caused the order to break up into different branches, of which the Friars Minor, the Conventuals, and the Capuchins still remain.

The women's branch was started by St. Clare (1193/94-1253), who founded the Monastery of San Damiano in Assisi in 1212 on the advice of Francis. Over the years, there developed the Clarists, the Grey Sisters, the Urbanists, the Colletins, the Conceptionists, the Annunciationists, and others.

J. MOORMAN, *A History of the Franciscan Order from its Origins to the Year 1517*, Oxford, 1968.
R. MANSELLI, *S. Francesco d'Assisi*, Rome, 1980. Translation in French by H. LOVETTE, *Saint François d'Assise*, Paris, 1981.
X., *Francesco d'Assisi nell'ottava centenario della nascita*, Milan, 1982.

117. On Mount Carmel in Palestine, near the Mediterranean Sea, hermits had lived a strict penitential life for centuries.

In the course of the twelfth century, a number of crusaders reestablished a monastery. Albert of Vercelli, Patriarch of Jerusalem, drew up a rule at their request in 1209 that was approved in 1226 by Pope Honorius III. This was the beginning of the Carmelites or the Brothers of the Blessed Virgin Mary. They spread rapidly throughout Palestine and Syria. With the invasion of the Turks, they crossed to Europe. The first community in Europe was founded in Valenciennes (in the County of Flanders) in 1235. The Brothers of the Blessed Virgin devoted themselves to apostolic work and, particularly, the spread of the spirit of prayer. In the fifteenth century, the order had more than a thousand communities.

Blessed John Soreth, General of the order, founded a woman's branch, which Nicholas V approved in 1425. The sisters maintained strict enclosure and devoted themselves totally to prayer and contemplation.

J. SMET, *The Carmelites. A History of the Brothers of Our Lady of Mount Carmel*, 4 vols., Darien, Illinois, 1975-1986.

118. Augustine (354-430), had founded communities in North Africa, in Hippo and Tagaste. After the Vandal invasions, the members settled on islands in the Mediterranean Sea, and some even sailed to Europe. In Italy, they called themselves the Hermits of Saint Augustine. They did not live independently but in communities just outside of the cities, and the groups had no juridical links with each other. In 1244, Innocent IV granted their request to assist them in their striving for unity and assigned as their guide the spirit and the way of life of Saint Augustine, which was already the case. Alexander IV united the monks by the bull *Licet Ecclesiae* of April 9, 1256, into one large order on the name of the Augustinian Hermits. He appointed a general, whom everyone had to obey. In 1257, the order received the privilege of exemption and also the privilege to beg. On October 3, 1567, Pius V officially recognized it as the fourth great mendicant order, even though it could acquire income and own property.

B. RANO, *The Order of Saint Augustine*, s.l., s.d.

The Dominicans, Franciscans, Carmelites, and Augustinians also established third orders (tertiaries) for lay people who lived in the world but still wanted to participate in the ideals and the strength of a particular order.

C) The Universities

119. Up until the thirteenth century, education was provided in chapter and abbey schools. With the rise of the free cities, another form of education developed. Dispensed clergy and students joined together in independent corporations that were recognized by the Church and the State. In 1231, Gregory IX granted them a separate status with their own rights and exemptions and placed them directly under papal authority.

These universities (*universitas magistrorum et scholarium*), which took over the scientific work from the monasteries, together with the mendicant orders, contributed to the unity, reform, and revival of Christian life.

The *European Republic of Teaching Clergy* was a powerful asset for the Pope. It supported and spread his theocratic ideas in the spirit of the Gregorian Reform. The pope founded most of the universities. By 1400, there were forty-four, some of them quite famous, such as Bologna (1088), Oxford (ca. 1200), Paris (1215), Padua (1222), Naples (1224), Toulouse (1229), Rome (1244/45), Salamanca (1255), Prague (1348), Vienna (1365), Heidelberg (1386), and Cologne (1388).

Great scholars taught at the universities, such as Albert the Great (1193-1280) and St. Thomas Aquinas (1225/1226-1274), who were Dominicans, and St. Bonaventure (1221-1274) and Duns Scotus (ca. 1260-1308), who were Franciscans.

J. VERGER, *Les Universités au Moyen Age,* P.U.F., S.U.P., section l'historien, no. 14, Paris, 1973. *The Universities in the Late Middle Ages. Les universités à la fin du Moyen-Age*, Louvain, 1980[2] (*Mediaevalia Lovaniensia,* ser. I, studia VI).

120. Bibliography

G. LE BRAS, *Institutions ecclésiastiques de la chrétienté médiévale (Histoire de l'Église,* A. FLICHE, V. MARTIN, XII, 2 vols), Paris, 1959-1964.
M.D. KNOWLES - D. OBOLENSKY, *The Christian Centuries. A New History of The Catholic Church, vol. II, The Middle Ages*, London-New York, 1972[2].
J. VERGER, *Les Universités au Moyen Age (L'Histoire,* XIV), Paris, 1973.
H. JEDIN, (ed.) *Die Mittelalterliche Kirche* (*Handbuch der Kirchengeschichte,* III, 1-2), Freiburg-Basel-Vienna, 1973[2].
W. ULLMANN, *A Short History of the Papacy in the Middle Ages*, London, 1974[2].
J. HOURLIER, *L'âge classique (1140-1378). Les religieux* (*Histoire du droit et des institutions de l'Église en Occident,* X), Paris, 1974.
F. PRINZ, *Mönchtum und Gesellschaft im Frühmittelalter* (*Wege der Forschung,* CCCXII), Darmstadt, 1976.

J. RICHARDS, *The Popes and the Papacy in the Early Middle Ages, 476-752*, London, 1979.

J. DELUMEAU (ed.), *Histoire vécue du peuple chrétien*, 2 vols., Toulouse, 1979.

F. RAPP, *L'Église et la vie religieuse en Occident à la fin du moyen âge* (*Nouvelle Clio*, XXV), Paris, 1980².

*The Universities in the Late Middle Ages. Les universités à la fin du moyen âge* (*Mediaevalia Lovaniensia*, series I, *studia* VI), Louvain, 1980².

A. SCHNEIDER - A. WIENAND, *Und Sie folgten den Regel St. Benedikts. Die Cistercienser und das benediktinische Mönchtum*, Cologne, 1981.

L. BUISSON, *Potestas und Caritas. Die päpstliche Gewalt im Spätmittelalter* (*Forschungen zur kirchlichen Rechtsgeschichte und zum Kirchenrecht*) Cologne - Vienna, 1982².

H.J. BERMAN, *Law and Revolution. The Formation of the Western Legal Tradition*, Cambridge, 1983.

K. PENNINGTON, *Pope and Bishops. The Papal Monarchy in the Twelfth and Thirteenth Centuries*, Philadelphia, 1984.

J. PAUL, *L'Église et la culture en Occident, IXe-XIIe siècles*. 2 vols. Paris, 1986.

N. HOUSLEY, *The Avignon Papacy and the Crusades, 1305-1378*, Oxford, 1986.

H. FUHRMANN, *Einladung ins Mittelalter*, Munich 1988.

D. KNOWLES, *The Evolution of Medieval Thought*, London-New York, 1988².

## Chapter II

# DOCUMENTARY SOURCES

A) Gregorian Collections

121. Gregory VII sought to reform the Church by again postulating papal primacy. At his behest, a consistent apparatus was constructed from which, on the basis of papal documents, all the writings that contradicted the Roman tradition were excluded. Even false *capitularia* and decretals were used for that purpose.

A useful collection in this sense is the *Liber canonum et decretorum Sanctorum Patrum* of which we possess three different manuscripts in Florence. The manuscript of the Central National Library, has been found in the Dominican Monastery of Santa Maria Novella, therefore called the *Collectio Santa Maria Novella*. It originated in Luca where it must have been put together in or before the pontificate of Gregory VII, thus somewhere between 1063 and 1083. Its 183 titles treat diciplinary matters of that period.

122. Around 1076, some unknown authors in Rome, probably members of the papal chancellery, and perhaps at the request of Hildebrand, compiled the *Collectio 74 titulorum* for the use of canon lawyers. It is the first attempt to formulate a theological and canonical codification on the Church and papal primacy by means of privileges, law, and dogmas. In addition, it secured the privileges and immunities of the regular and secular clergy and set the norms for the selection and consecration of bishops and the ordination of priests. The collection became the handbook of the Roman curia, of the popes, and of their apostolic legates, who, with the help of this book, introduced the principles of the reform in all the Western countries. The *Collectio IV Librorum* of 1085 completes and classifies the previous work.

## Editions

J. MOTTA, *Liber canonum diversorum sanctorum patrum sive Collectio in CLXXXIII titulos digesta* (*Monumenta iuris canonici*, series B: *Corpus collectionum*, vol. 7), Città del Vaticano, 1988, LXVII-391 p.

J.T. GILCHRIST, *Diversorum patrum sententie sive collectio in 74 titulos digesta* (*Monumenta Iuris Canonici*, ser. B. Vol. 1), Città del Vaticano, 1973.

## Studies

G. FRANSEN, "Autour de la collection en 74 titres," *Revue de droit canonique* 25 (1975), pp. 61-73.

J. GILCHRIST, "The Relationship Between the Collection in Four Books and the Collection in Seventy-Four Titles," *Bulletin of Medieval Canon Law* 11 (1982), pp. 13-30.

ID., "The Manuscripts of the Canonical Collection in Four Books," *Zeitschrift der Savigny Stiftung für Rechtsgeschichte. Kanonistische Abteilung* 69 (1983), pp. 64-120.

123. Around 1083, Anselmus Lucensis, Bishop of Lucca († 1086), wrote a work containing thirteen books with 1150 chapters that contained the entirety of canon law in a logical order. Its logical and methodical order, excelling by far that of the previous collections, and the new presentation earned his work widespread approval, and it exercised considerable influence on subsequent collections and the polemical writings in the investiture struggle. This has led Stickler to conclude: "Collectio Anselmi facile princeps collectionum Gregorianarum iudicari potest simulac caput eminens in historia collectionum iuris canonici" (*op. cit.*, p. 172).

## Edition

F. THANER, *Anselmi episcopi Lucensis collectio canonum una cum collectione minore*, 2 vols. in 1, Innsbruck, 1906-1915 (anastatic reprint, Aalen, 1965).

124. The *collectio canonum* of Cardinal Deusdedit (Dieudonné) († ca. 1100) was compiled between 1083 and 1086. It does not contain all the texts on ecclesiastical reform, but only those that illustrated and justified the juridically privileged position of

the Church such as those on simony, celibacy, ecclesiastical property, and the obligation of the secular princes to assist in the imposition and execution of penalties. Its influence, however, was not great.

Edition

V. WOLF VON GLANVELL, *Die Kanonessammlung des Kardinals Deusdedit*, Paderborn, 1905 (anastatic reprint, Aalen, 1967).

125. In the post-Gregorian period, the canonical activitity was particularly intense during the pontificate of Pope Urban II (1088-1099). A fine example of this period is the *Collectio Britannica* of the British Museum, most probably put together in Rome around 1090 or after the pontificate of Gregory VII. It contains 233 letters of the popes, from Gelasius I up to Urbanus II, and texts from the institutions of Justinianus and the Pandects, the Collectio Deusdedit and the Fathers. The most famous canonist of the eleventh century was Yves Carnutensis (ca. 1040-1116), provost of the regular canons of Saint Augustine at Saint-Quentin and Bishop of Chartres from 1091 to 1116. Between 1093 and 1095, he wrote a three-volume standard work: the *collectio trium partium* or *Tripartita*, the *Decretum*, and the *Panormia*.

The first part of the *Tripartita* gives, in chronological order, 655 papal decretals from St. Clement to Urban II. The second part contains 789 fragments from Eastern, African, French, and Spanish councils. Between the Greek and the African councils, there are twenty-nine passages from Greek ecclesiastical writers under the title *Sententiae Graecorum doctorum*, and also extracts from monastic rules of the West and from the writings of the Fathers. The third part is an abbreviated and more convenient edition of the *Decretum*, cf. below, and is divided into twenty-nine titles.

The *Decretum* contains 3760 fragments in seventeen volumes. Carnutensis made considerable use of the decree of Burchard of Worms, of the first two volumes of his *Tripartita*, and of texts of the Fathers and Church writers, but without any order or method.

The *Panormia* is an abbreviated version of his decree for the use of the clergy in practice. It consists of a foreword and eight books and contains all the necessary rules, organized very methodically. In addition, the chapters — to facilitate their use — are generally preceded by *summaria* that present a legal rule in precise language. Thus, the *Panormia* can rightly be called a concise encyclopedia of canon law. The exceptionally large number of manuscript copies are proof of its great authority and influence. The only useful edition is the one printed by Sebastian Brant in 1499.

If these three works are not of Yves' sole authorship, they would have been, in any case, the work of students who worked under his impulse and inspiration. The *Decretum* and the *Panormia* form volume 161 of the *Patrologia Latina*.

126. Yves of Chartres was a moderate canonist. He defended the superiority of the spiritual power, but held that the salvation of mankind could only be achieved through good cooperation between Church and State (*le monde bien gouverné*) and in the unity of Church and State. "Il ne saurait y avoir de bon gouvernement là où il n'y a union entre la royauté et le sacerdoce", he wrote to Henry I, King of England. In contrast to Burchard of Worms, he did not hesitate to give the decrees of Christian princes the force of law on the condition that they were not in conflict with the doctrine of the Church. In his works, he mixed rules of Roman Law and of the *capitularia*, authentic and inauthentic, of the Frankish kings with the purely canonical rules. In so doing, he emphasized and the necessity of cooperation and unity between Church and State, and the fervent bond between civil jurists and canonists. It was mostly through his efforts that Roman Law became known North of the Alps.

Studies

R. Sprandel, *Ivo von Chartres und seine Stellung in der Kirchengeschichte*, Stuttgart, 1962.

Both in and out of Italy, there was an abundance of local collections up to 1140, either under the influence of the Gregorian Reform or dependent on Yves Carnutensis. Cf. P. Fournier - G. Le Bras, *Histoire des collections canoniques en Occident*, vol. II, Paris, 1932 (anastatic reprint, Aalen, 1972), pp. 115-313.

B) The *Decretum Gratiani*

127. Little is known about Gratian. He was probably born at the end of the eleventh century in Chiusi in Tuscany and died in Bologna around 1160. He was a theologian and also an expert in canon law. He taught in Bologna. There, in the monastery of Saints Nabor and Felix, between 1130 and 1140, he composed his rubrics. For centuries, he was thought to have been a Camaldolese monk of this monastery, but this has been definitely disproved by John T. Noonan.[1] It is generally accepted that Gratian was the first who taught canon law as an autonomous science. He distinguished theology from canon law and is called *Pater scientiae canonicae*. Around 1140 (according to a recent author: between 1125-1140), he completed in Bologna his *Decretum Gratiani*, which made him one of the most renowned canonists of all time.[2] From the title he gave to his work, *Concordia discordantium canonum*, his intention was clear. It was to resolve the *discordantia* or contradictions that occurred so often in the innumerable sources by bringing these texts in harmony with each other (*concordare*) and thus to establish fixed law.

It is certainly not a *concordantia*, a compilation of parallel texts, as it was called at the end of the twelfth century. In any event, it enjoyed widespread approval, so that it was even entitled

---

[1] J.T. NOONAN recently demonstrated that Gratian was not a Camaldulens of this monastery; J.T. NOONAN, "Gratian slept here: The Changing Identity of the Father of the Systematic Study of Canon Law," *Traditio* 35 (1979), pp. 145-172. See also C. MESINI, "Postille sulla biografia del "magister Gratianus" padre del diritto canonico," *Apollinaris* 54 (1981), pp. 509-537.

[2] G. FRANSEN, *La date du décret de Gratien*, in *Revue d'histoire ecclésiastique* 51 (1956), pp. 521-531; P. LANDAU, *Quellen und Bedeutung des Gratianischen Dekrets*, in *Studia et documenta historiae et iuris* 52 (1986), pp. 218-235.

*Corpus iuris canonici, corpus decretorum,* or *Liber canonum.* Generally, however, the title *Decretum* was used according to the example of Yves of Chartres and Burchard of Worms, whose works it replaced.

128. The *Decretum Gratiani* introduced a completely new era in the history of canon law. Not only did it replace the preceding decrees but it also provided a systematic and logical ordering of documents taken from existing collections supplemented by prescriptions of the popes Pascal II (1099-1118) and Innocent II (1130-1143) and of the Second Lateran Council (1139). Thus, as Stickler rightly noted, the *Decretum Gratiani* inaugurated an entirely new period: "Decreto Gratiani nova epocha evolutionis iuris incipit; est terminus ad quem, finis, et terminus a quo, initium" (pp. 217 and 201). It combined all the previous collections, thus forming a basis for later collections. Until the promulgation of the first *Codex Iuris Canonici* in 1917, it remained a true standard work of canon law. Prior to the middle of the twelfth century, there had existed only systematic collections of church prescriptions, but no treatment of canon law in its entirety as a theoretical exposition. With his *Decretum,* Gratian published the first synthesis of the universally applicable canon law. At the same time, he provided the later popes with a foundation upon which their *litterae decretales* could rest.

129. Gratian worked with a set method. He first supplemented the *concordia* with *paragraphi*, which were later called *dicta Gratiani*. They contain an explanation of the various texts: "solutio significatione, solutio loco, solutio tempore, solutio dispensatione seu exceptione." In addition, he included *auctoritates*, in which he cited arguments to support his choice of a particular thesis, "Quellenstellen." Furthermore, numerous texts from Justinian law are also included in his text. He ordered all these texts methodically, placed them in their context, tested them for origin and *raison d'être*, compared them with each other, interpreted them juridically, and combined them to form a logically ordered whole. Cf. P. Andrieu-Guitrancourt, *op. cit.*, p. 742.

130. In Gratian's work, three parts may be clearly distinguished, but Gratian himself did not assign them titles. The first part deals with the sources of the law (dist. 1-20), which Van Hove (p. 340) called the introduction. It also treats divergent subjects, primarily concerning the ecclesiastical hierarchy and the clergy (dist. 21-101). The *distictiones* are divided into *canones*.

The second part is divided into thirty-six *causae* and subdivided into *quaestiones*. It is generally accepted that Gratian did this himself. It deals with procedure, secular property, religious orders, marriage, and confession. The last part is generally entitled *De consacratione* because it groups the rules on the sacraments, excepting marriage, and sacramentals.

The subdivisions of Part 1 into 101 *distinctiones* and of Part 3 into five *distinctiones* are probably of a later date. It is supposed that this was done by Gratian's student, Paucapalea.[1]

131. According to his student, Gratian's own additions, as well as several later ones, were called *paleae*. The glossators also used this term for some superfluous textual repetitions from the hand of Gratian himself. As a professor in Bologna, Paucapalea added 166 *auctoritates* to the original text sometime before 1148. This is the oldest commentary on the decree. Paucapalea delved into texts that were older than the decree itself, even texts of Roman law, in his efforts to authenticate Gratian's doctrine.

Innumerable manuscript copies of the *Decretum Gratiani* and many editions are still available. The best known are certainly those of Jean Chappuis and Vitalis de Thebis (Paris, 1500 and 1503), the *Correctores Romani* (Rome 1582), the brothers Petrus and Franciscus Pithou (Paris, 1687), Justus Henning Böhmer (Halle, 1747), Aemilius Ludovicus Richter (Leipzig, 1839), and Aemilius Friedberg (Leipzig, 1879, anastatic reprint in Leipzig in 1922 and 1928 and in Graz in 1955 and 1959).

---

[1] Plan, cfr A. STICKLER, *o.c.*, pp. 205-207; P. ANDRIEU-GUITRANCOURT, *o.c.*, pp. 743-746. — about the rules for quoting, cfr A. VAN HOVE, *o.c.*, no. 345; A. STICKLER, *o.c.*, pp. 215-216; W.M. PLÖCHL, *o.c.*, vol. II, p. 473, most recently: $D_1$ c.1; C. 1 q.1 c.1; D1 c1 *de consecratione*, and in some cases: c.1 D.1 *de consecratione*.

132. In spite of the renown and the great authority of the *Decretum Gratiani*, it remained a private collection with no universal force of law. The ecclesiastical authorities never officially recognized or approved the collection, so every text included in it retained the value that it had independently of it.

However, no text was abrogated by the *Decretum*. Nevertheless, some of the texts, even the *dicta*, acquired the force of universally applicable law, even though they rested on false or private sources. The *Decretum* was publicly and generally taught in the schools, enriched with glosses, summaries, and commentaries, and used by popes and tribunals in the drafting and application of laws. This universal and manifold use, however, did not change its private character. P. Gasparri confirmed this in the foreword to the 1917 CIC: "Gratiani decreto publica nullo tempore accessit auctoritas... illud... Apostolica Sedes numquam... authenticum declaravit, nec legis... contulit..." This was repeated in the foreword to the Codex of 1983: "item privato inceptu a monacho Gratiano."

133. Bibliography

A. VAN HOVE, *De oorsprong van de kerkelijke rechtswetenschap en de scholastiek. Mededelingen van de koninklijke Vlaamse academie voor wetenschappen, letteren en schone kunsten van België*, 1946.
J. DE GHELLINCK, *Le mouvement théologique du XII$^e$ siècle*, Bruxelles-Paris, 1948.
L. SANTIFALLER - F. EHEIM, "Die Handschriften des Decretum Gratiani in der Wiener Nationalbibliothek," *Österreichisches Archiv für Kirchenrecht* 2 (1951), pp. 82-89.
*Studia Gratiana*, Bologna-Rome, from 1953 on.
P. LANDAU, "Gratian (von Bologna)," *Theologische Realenzyklopädie*, vol. 14, Berlin-New York, 1985, pp. 124-130.
S. KUTTNER, "Gratian," *Dictionnaire d'histoire et de géographie ecclésiastiques*, vol. 21, 1986, col. 1235-1239.
P. LANDAU, "Quellen und Bedeutung des Gratianischen Dekrets," *Studia et documenta historiae et iuris* 52 (1986), pp. 218-235.

## C) The *Quinque Compilationes Antiquae*

134. In the twelfth century, the prestige and the power of the popes steadily increased as a result of the Gregorian Reform. The popes were asked to resolve problems in every domain of society.

The interventions of the popes generally took place by means of decretals, which often had great juridical value. Indeed, several popes of this period were significant canonists. Alexander III (1159-1181) and Innocent III (1198-1216) were particularly active not only as advisors but also as legislators.

The texts not retained in the *Decretum Gratiani* and the more recent ones, were called the *capitula extravagantia* or the *extra Decretum*. They were considered not to be part of the *Decretum* itself, but additional *paleae*. At about the time of the third Lateran Council (1179), separate collections were made up for them, called *collectiones capitulorum*, or *collectiones decretalium*. See A. Stickler, *op. cit.*, pp. 221-225, 229-232.

Five collections, commonly called the *Quinque compilationes antiquae*, met with a relative degree of success and even served as the model for later collections.

135. The *Compilatio prima* was formed by the *Breviarium extravagantium (decretalium)* of Bernardus Baldus Papiensis of Pavia. It was compiled between 1187 and 1191 when Bernardus was provost of the cathedral chapter of Pavia. Around 1172, he had already made a systematic collection of decretals of the popes from Honorius II (1124-1130) to Alexander III (1159-1181) under the name *Collectio Parisiensis*. Thereafter, he worked until 1187 at the Roman curia. In 1191, he became bishop of Faenza and in 1198 of Pavia, where he died on 18 September 1213.

With his *Breviarium*, Bernardus Papiensis set out to assemble all the texts not included in the *Decretum*, both those not used by Gratian as well as later ones, and to organize them to facilitate administration and study. The *Breviarium*, in addition to the decretals up to Clement III (1191), also contains canons of ecumenical and local councils, fragments from the Church Fathers and ecclesiastical writers, and Roman and Germanic laws. Bernardus' work consists of five books, each divided into titles and further subdivided into chapters (*capitula*). Bernardus was the first compiler to use the Roman law division (cf. *Codex Iustiniani*), which henceforth will also be applied in canon law collections.

He divided his work into five parts: 1) the constitutive sources of the law and the ecclesiastical hierarchy, 2) the legal organization and procedure *in contentiosis*, 3) the clergy (secular, regular), benefices, churches, associations, temporal property, contracts, 4) marriage, and 5) penal law (crimes and penalties) and procedure *in criminalibus*. This division originated in the Roman Law division of *personae, res,* and *actiones* and was simply referred to by later glossators as *iudex, iudicium, clerus, connubium, crimen*.

The *Breviarium* turned out to be very valuable and influential, as shown by its general use in universities, jurisprudence, and administration. Thus, it was greatly enriched with glosses. Bernardus himself composed a summary when he was bishop of Faenza, the *Summa titulorum*; cf. the edition of E.A.T. Laspeyres, Regensburg, 1860. Moreover, it was most probably the model for the *Saksenspiegel*, a medieval law book completed around 1225 by Eike von Repgau (Repgow) (1180/90-1233). Nevertheless, the collection never attained an official character. Cf. G. Fransen, "Les diverses formes de la compilatio prima," in *Scrinium Lovaniense* Gembloux, 1961, pp. 235-253.

136. On 28 December 1210, Innocent III (1198-1216), with the bull *Devotioni vestrae*, promulgated the *Compilatio tertia*, which had been written by Petrus Collivaccinus or Beneventanus at his command. It was sent to the University of Bologna to be used in court as well as in teaching: "tam in iudiciis quam in scholis." This collection became the first official collection of decretals. It contains decretals from the first twelve years of the pontificate of Innocent III, from 1198 to 1209, and is divided into 122 titles with 482 chapters. Although it is the second collection chronologically, it is only third as regards content, so that it was called the *compilatio tertia* by later canonists.

137. Joannes Gallensis from Wales wrote the *Compilatio secunda* between 1210 and 1215. He compiled decretals from Clement III (1187-1191) and Celestine III (1191-1198), and added a few prescriptions "forgotten" in the *Compilatio I*. Thus, he filled the gap between the *Breviarium* and the *Compilatio III*. The collection consists of 106 titles and 331 chapters. However, this collection was never officially recognized.

138. The remaining decretals of Innocent III were assembled with a few earlier decretals and with the canons of the Fourth Lateran Council (1215) by Joannes Teutonicus († 1245/46) to form the *Compilatio quarta*. It consists of sixty-nine titles and 189 chapters. Innocent III refused to promulgate it, so Joannes Teutonicus published it after the Pope died (16 July 1216), presumably in the second half of 1216 or the beginning of 1217. The doctors of Bologna were initially suspicious of this quasi-official work. However, general use and the great respect that Joannes Teutonicus enjoyed led to it being recognized as the *compilatio quarta* or *Liber quattuor decretalium*.

139. Tancredus, finally, was responsible for the *Compilatio quinta*. It contains decretals from Honorius III from 1216 to 1226 and the imperial constitution of Frederick II of November 22, 1220, on the privileges of the Church. Like the *Compilatio tertia*, this collection was also solemnly promulgated by Pope Honorius III with the bull *Novae Causarum* of May 2, 1226. It consists of 94 titles and 223 chapters. It is the second authentic collection of decretals.

140. With the *Decretum Gratiani* and the *Quinque compilationes antiquae*, scholars and practitioners had a readily available set of texts that comprised the positive law of the Church of the time. Among the numerous editions, we name those by Friedberg:

E. FRIEDBERG, *Die Canones-Sammlungen zwischen Gratian und Bernard von Pavia*, Leipzig, 1897 (anastatic reprint, Graz, 1958).
E. FRIEDBERG, *Quinque compilationes antiquae*, Leipzig, 1882 (anastatic reprint, Graz, 1956).

D) The Decretals of Gregory IX (*liber extra* = X) 1234

141. For practice and for education, the *Decretum Gratiani* and the *Quinque compilationes antiquae* (1191-1226) formed the principal sources. However, six different collections had to be consulted and these, although they offered an enormous number of texts, overlapped and even contradicted each other. Indeed, the decretals promulgated later amended the previous ones or abrogated them in whole or in part (*abrogabant vel derogabant*). These collections also cited local norms that did not or could not form the universal law of the Church. Thus, uncertainty remained about the law in force. In addition, there were also several texts that did not appear in any of these collections but that still contained valid legal norms. They were often used by teachers and judges.

All this greatly complicated the teaching and application of canon law. Therefore, Pope Gregory IX (1227-1241), who was elected at the age of 80, decided to have a new, uniform, and simplified compilation made that would contain only the laws in force. For the compilation of these *Decretales Gregorii IX* he appointed Raymond of Penafort, a Dominican and professor in civil and canon law in Bologna.

Raymond of Penafort was born around 1180 in Penafort near Barcelona. He studied philosophy and theology in Barcelona and civil and canon law in Bologna, where he became a professor. In 1223, he joined the Dominicans. Gregory IX called him to Rome in 1230, where he worked on the collection for four years. He returned to Barcelona in 1236, to become general of his order in 1238. He died in 1275, at about the age of 95. Clement VIII canonized him in 1601.

142. The task of Raymond of Penafort was threefold. He had to eliminate all the abrogated laws, all the superfluous explanations that were interspersed in the texts, and all repetitions. Then he had to improve the texts as he saw fit, and even change or add to them if he considered it necessary. For this purpose, Pope Gregory IX promulgated at Raymond's request several decretals "ad dubia

solvenda et quaestiones elucidandas." Thus, after the *Decretum Gratiani*, Raymond of Penafort ordered all of papal law.

He based himself primarily on the *Quinque Compilationes Antiquae*, from which he took 1756 chapters of the 2139. To them he added seven decretals of Innocent III and two of unknown origin. He also consulted the *Canones Apostolorum*, the documents of the ecumenical councils, particularly those of Lateran III and IV, writings of the Fathers and ecclesiastical writers, and even the compilations of Germanic and Roman civil law. He concluded with the 195 decretals of Gregory IX, both the previous ones and the ones that had been promulgated at his request.

Raymond of Penafort structured his work in a logical order. All the legal problems were placed in the five classic rubrics of the *Compilatio prima*, each rubric comprising one volume: *iudex, iudicium, clerus, connubia, crimen*. Each book was also divided into titles and the titles into chapters.

143. On 5 September 1234, Gregory IX promulgated the new collection in his bull *Rex pacificus* and sent it to the University of Bologna and probably also to that of Paris. It thus became the first official publication of canon law and it remained the most important collection until the 1917 Code. The Pope also declared that all other collections were void and prescribed that only these decretals would be used in schools and tribunals, and forbade new compilations without the express permission of the Holy See.

Therefore, the *Decretales Gregorii IX* formed an authentic, universally applicable collection with an exclusive value. All the texts that were included received, irrespective of their origin, the force of law (authenticity) and applied to the entire Church community (universality). Moreover, all former legal texts, whether or not they were in private or public compilations, lost their force of law (exclusivity). The *Decretum Gratiani* did retain its moral value, so that it was still commonly used in the teaching of law and by tribunals in spite of its private character.

144. The work had no title at its promulgation, so it is generally called the *Decretales Gregorii IX* or the *Codex Gregoria-*

*nus* after its sponsor. Other titles included *Liber sextus* as a continuation of the *Quinque compilationes antiquae*, or the *Liber extravagantium* or, in short, the *Liber extra*, as a supplement to the *Corpus Iuris Canonici* of the time or *the Decretum Gratiani*. For convenience sake, it is simply quoted as "X."[1]

145. There are about a thousand remaining manuscripts of the *Decretales Gregorii IX*. The first printed edition is from Mainz and dates from 1473. Pope Gregory XIII (1572-1585) instructed the *Correctores Romani* to revise the text by correcting and verifying it. They delegated this task to Franciscus Pegna and Sixtus Fabri. On 1 July 1580, Gregory XIII declared the text edited by these two men to be authentic so that no additions, omissions, or changes were permitted. In 1582, it was published as a part of the *Editio Romana*, which also contained the *Liber Sextus*, the *Clementinae*, and the *Extravagantes*. Later editions were provided by the brothers P. and F. Pithou, by J.H. Böhmer, and Aemilius L. Richter. The best known is that of Aemilius Friedberg, which was published in Leipzig in 1881. Anastatic reprints were published in 1922 and 1928 in Leipzig and in 1955 and 1959 in Graz.

E) *Liber Sextus Bonifatii VIII* (1298)

146. However ambitiously conceived and complete the *Decretales Gregorii IX* might have been, they did not escape the changed spirit of the times. Gregory IX's successors, Innocent IV (1243-1254), Gregory X (1271-1276), and Nicholas III (1277-1280), promulgated *novae* or *novellae constitutiones, novellae Gregorianae* and quoted them in authentic collections. Several private collections of the approximately one hundred and fifty remaining decretals appeared. Inevitably, ambiguities, repetitions, and contradictions again occurred. Therefore, Boniface VIII (1294-1303) decided to collect the "extravagant" decretals in a new collection. He

---

[1] On rules for quoting, cf. A. VAN HOVE, *op. cit.*, no. 363 (p. 359); A. STICKLER, *op. cit.*, pp. 250-251; W.M. PLOCHL, *op. cit.*, vol. II p. 479, and according to recent quotations: X,1,2,3 (= *liber extra*, book 1, title 2, chapter 1). Succeeding collections are quoted accordingly, e.g. VI (*liber sextus*), 1,2,3; Clem, 1,2,3.

changed the old legal texts into new norms and grouped them according to the structure of the *Liber Extra*.

147. The *Liber Sextus* —as Boniface VIII called his collection— consisted predominantly (two-thirds) of his own decretals (251 chapters) alongside those of his predecessors and the canons of the councils of Lyons (1245 and 1274). As a supplement, it also contained the eighty-eight *regulae iuris* of Roman law of Dinus Mugellanus or de Rossonis, a jurist from Bologna. These were thought to be useful for the interpretation, application, and extension of ecclesiastical norms.

148. By virtue of its promulgation in the bull *Sacrosanctae Romanae Ecclesiae* of 3 March 1298 and its transmission to the universities of Bologna, Paris, and others, this supplement to the five books of Gregory IX received an authentic and universal character. However, the work has only relative exclusivity. Of all the norms that were promulgated after the *Decretales Gregorii IX* (i.e., after September 6, 1234 and before December 24, 1294), only those that were included in the *Liber Sextus* retained their validity. The bull also suppressed the universal laws of the *Liber Extra* that conflicted with a stipulation of the *Liber Sextus*. This was in accordance with the ancient adagium: *Lex posterior derogat priori, nisi expresse aliud dicatur*.

149. From the fifteenth century onwards, many publishers profited greatly from the *Liber Sextus*. The *Editio Romana* of 1582, which provided the official text, is considered to be the principal edition. The last critical edition was that of Aemilius Friedberg of Leipzig in 1881. Anastatic reprints of it have been produced in Leipzig (1922 and 1928) and Graz (1955 and 1959).

F) *Constitutiones Clementinae* (1317)

150. After 1298, private collections were again made of the constitutions of Boniface VIII (for the period from 1298 to 1303) and of Benedict XI (1303-1304) under the name *Constitutiones extravagantes Libri Sexti*. Indeed, these popes were no less legisla-

tively active than was Gregory IX in their concern to provide a legal framework for the rapid evolution of society.

151. Clement V (1305-1314) ignored these private collections in the compilation of his *Liber Septimus*. Clement included only his own constitutions which he had promulgated occasionally or at the time of the Council of Vienne (1311-1312). Clement V promulgated his collection on 21 March 1314, but he died before he could send them to the universities of Orléans and Paris. Therefore, the Roman Curia considered them insufficiently promulgated and thus without force of law.

152. Pope John XXII (1316-1334) ordered the work revised and issued it on his own authority on October 25, 1317 with the bull *Quoniam nulla*. It was sent to the universities of Bologna and Paris.

Although Clement V and John XXII used the method that was applied in the Gregorian collection of decretals and the *Liber Sextus*, not all the norms promulgated after the *Liber Sextus* were included. These norms retained their power of law insofar as they were not in conflict with the compilation, so it lost even relative exclusivity. The glossators therefore called it simply the *Constitutiones Clementinae*. It did not deserve to be known as a *liber Septimus* in the sequence of the supplements to the *Decretum Gratiani*. These acts were published by the same publishers as those of the previous collections.

153. After the *Clementinae*, only two authentic collections were promulgated, the first volume of the *Bullarium* of Benedict XIV and the acts of Pius X (1903-1914) up until 1908. The latter were published in five volumes in Rome from 1905 to 1913. The *Codex Iuris Canonici* of 1917 is the first complete collection thereafter.

G) The *Extravagantes*

154. Even after the *Constitutiones Clementinae*, there remained uncodified, generally applicable decretals, since Boniface VIII

issued decretals in addition to his *Liber Sextus*, and the *Clementinae* could not claim exclusivity. Moreover, the succeeding popes also legislated a great deal. Up to the end of the fifteenth century, *extravagantes* or private collections were developed. They differed from each other in content, ordering, and importance, so a systematic compilation appeared to be required. Two Parisian publishers therefore asked Joannes Chappuis and Vitalis de Thebis in 1499 to prepare the text for the *Corpus Iuris Canonici*. They compiled the *extravagantes* in two separate collections. In their first work, the *Extravagantes Joannis XXII*, they systematically brought together twenty decretals, promulgated by John XXII between 1317 and 1324 under fourteen titles and twenty chapters. To this they added the glosses of Zenzelinus de Cassanis from Montpellier.

The *Extravagantes Communes* contain seventy generally accepted (*communiter occurrentes et traditae, ideoque receptae*) decretals and constitutions from Urban IV (1261-1264) to Sixtus IV (1471-1484). In the second edition (1503) of what was called the *Corpus Iuris Canonici*, they included four additional decretals.

155. Neither of these two collections could claim authenticity. The decretals included in them derive their force of law from their original promulgations and thus independently of their inclusion. The only authority they received from the collections was a moral one.

Edition

J. TARRANT, *Extravagantes Joannis XXII*, Città del Vaticano, 1983 (*Monumenta iuris canonici*, ser. B, Vol. 6).

156. The name *Corpus Iuris Canonici*, which indicates the entirety of the collections of canon law, was applied very early, occasionally even for the *Decretum Gratiani*. Gregory XIII in 1582 had an official edition published in Rome in which the five collections (*Decretum Gratiani, Decretales Gregorii IX, Liber Sextus, Clementinae, Extravagantes*) were combined, but without a

common title, although he did call the collection the *Corpus Iuris Canonici*. The title appeared for the first time in the Frankfurt edition of 1586.

Edition

E. FRIEDBERG, *Corpus Iuris Canonici*, 2 vols., Leipzig, 1876-1882² (anastatic reprint, Graz, 1955 and 1959).

H) Other collections

157. Not only the decretals of popes were compiled, and even so their acts and letters with dispensations, privileges, and benefices.

The *Regesta* or *Registra* started in Rome in the fourth century. Initially, a chronological order was used, but later on, more systematic methods were introduced, and the subject matter became the criterion for division. Almost all of the earlier *regesta*, that is, up to Innocent III (1198-1216), have been lost, but the later ones have been preserved to a large extent.

From the nineteenth century on, these collections of letters attracted more attention because of editions such as the *Regesta Pontificum Romanorum a condita Ecclesia ad annum post Christum natum 1196*, (Berlin, 1851, of Philipp Jaffé 2nd expanded and improved edition, 2 vols., Leipzig, 1885-1888; anastatic reprint, Graz, 1956) and the *Regesta Pontificum Romanorum inde ab anno post Christum natum 1198 ad annum 1304*, 2 vols. (Berlin, 1874-1875, anastatic reprint, Graz, 1957) of August Potthast. Both editions use the letters of several popes, and thus, together with the comments of the compilers, give a clear picture of the spirit of that time, and of the lives, and the works of the popes. Later editions supplement them; cf. A. Stickler, *op. cit.*, pp. 306-316.

«In his duobus operibus (Jaffé-Potthast) non exhibentur documenta integra RR. Pontificum, sed summaria excerpta tantum i.e. indicationes circa vitam RR. Pontificum, tempus expeditionis litterarum, locum a quo, personam ad quem, materiam de qua cum brevibus excerptis textus ipsius, si praecipui est momenti vel nondum editus. In fine uniuscuiusque acti adduntur indicationes operum et locorum, ubi textus integer editus invenitur» (A. STICKLER, *o.c.*, p. 309).

The papal letters of this period can be found in such editions as the *Epistulae Pontificum Romanorum ineditae* for the years 493 to 1198, Leipzig, 1885 (anastatic reprint, Graz, 1959) of S. Loewenfeld, and in the *Acta Pontificum Romanorum inedita* for the years 97 to 1198, (3 vols., Tübingen-Stuttgart, 1881-1886, anastatic reprint, Graz, 1958) of J. von Pflugh-Harttung, but principally in the *bullaria*, which will be discussed in detail below (cf. nos. 200-205).

158. The canons and decrees of the councils of the Lateran (four from 1123 to 1215, the fifth in 1512-1517), of Lyons (1245 and 1274), of Vienne (1311-1312), of Constance (1414-1418), and Basel (1431-1443) were included in separate collections in addition to being cited in decretal collections, cf. below, nrs. 206-211.

159. In the Rules of the Apostolic Chancery, chanceries and tribunals have directives for the writing of letters with dispensations, privileges, gifts, benefices, indulgences, delegations, and so on.

Pope John XXII (1316-1334) was the first pope to issue a relatively complete apparatus with seventy-two rules. Initially, each successive pope issued new rules for his pontificate "*ad modum edicti perpetui magistratus Romanorum.*" Gradually, these rules came to be approved and reissued by succeeding pontiffs. Since Clement XI (1700-1721), they have remained unchanged from pope to pope until Pius X ordered a revision on September 29, 1908.

Edition

E. von Ottenthal, *Regulae Cancellariae Apostolicae. Die päpstlichen Kanzleiregeln von Johannes XXII bis Nikolaus V, gesammelt und herausgegeben*, Innsbruck, 1888 (anastatic reprint, Aalen, 1968).

160. Finally, we must mention the concordats, the agreements that regulate the relationships between the Church and the State. In this period, the concordats of Worms (1122), Constance

(1418), Vienna (1448), and Bologna (1472 and 1516) are of great importance.

161. *Summary*

With the first official codification of canon law, the *Decretales Gregorii IX* of 1234, the new law, the law of the popes, entered the Church, and the classic era of canon law began. Nevertheless, these decretals did not abrogate the old law of the *Decretum Gratiani* (1140). Neither did the later official codifications of Boniface VIII in 1298 and John XXII in 1317. Noteworthy is the merger of private and official intiatives into a harmonious whole. Alongside their official collections, the popes tolerated private collections such as the *Extravagantes Joannis XXII* and the *Extravagantes communes*. This is a good illustration of the power of the popes of the thirteenth and fourteenth centuries. They put their stamp even on the canon law collections of our century, the *Codices Iuris Canonici* of 1917 and 1983. Modern canon law, which is the logical extension of their work, cannot be understood without an insight into these historical sources.

It is not surprising, therefore, that both Codes stipulate in Canon 6 that the laws taken from the old law have to be understood in the light of the canonical tradition.

162. Bibliography of the Second Period (Documentary Sources)

P. TORQUEBIAU - G. MOLLAT, "Corpus Iuris Canonici," *Dictionnaire de droit canonique*, vol. IV, 1949, col. 610-644.
G. LE BRAS - CH. LEFÈBVRE - J. RAMBAUD, *L'âge classique, 1140-1378* (*Histoire du droit et des institutions de l'Église en Occident*, vol. VII), Paris, 1965.
P. OURLIAC - H. GILLES, *La période postclassique (1378-1500)*, I, *La problématique de l'époque. Les sources* (*Histoire du droit et des institutions de l'Église en Occident*, vol. XIII), Paris, 1971.
P. ANDRIEU - GUITRANCOURT, *o.c.*, pp. 706-779.
A. STICKLER, *o.c.*, pp. 197-276.
W.M. PLÖCHL, *o.c.*, vol. II, pp. 465-488.

G. Fransen, "Les décrétales et les collections de décrétales," *Typologie des sources du Moyen-Age occidental*, vol. 2), Turnhout, 1972, 45 p. (complete edition, 1985).

K.W. Nörr, "Die Entwicklung des Corpus Iuris Canonici," *Handbuch der Quellen und Literatur der neueren europäischen Privatrechtsgeschichte*, vol. I, *Mittelalter*, München, 1973, pp. 835-846.

A. Giacobbi, *o.c.*, pp. 157-182.

J.F. von Schulte, *o.c.*, vol. I, pp. 39-91.

CHAPTER III

# THE SCIENCE OF LAW AND ITS PRACTITIONERS

A) Decretists

163. In the schools of canon law of the universities of Bologna, Paris, Pavia, and so on, professors studied the *Decretum Gratiani* exegetically and scholastically. Thus, they came to be known as "decretists." These decretists attempted to resolve contradictions by means of references to similar texts and produced a summary of the entire doctrine containing the general norms. The oldest textual studies consisted purely of *glossae*, which ultimately develop into true *commentaria*.

164. In the eighth century, jurists made notes in various manuscripts concerning individual words in order to clarify passages of the text. Depending on the place or origin, the *glossae* were called interlinear (between the lines), marginal (in the margin), authentic (with the words of the law itself), or magistral (according to an interpretation of the *doctores*). The entirety of such glosses formed an *apparatus glossarum*, and the writers are called glossators.

The glosses on one and the same work that were generally accepted as the most complete and the most correct were compiled to form a *glossa ordinaria*. It was a convenient tool for schools and tribunals, and generally enjoyed great authority. It sometimes became in turn the object of other glosses and commentaries, which closely followed the evolution of the law.

165. Initially, the decretists limited themselves only to glosses in the *Decretum Gratiani*. Paucapalea, Gratian's student, has the honor of being the first glossator (between 1140 and 1149).

In his footsteps followed Rolandus[1]. Other well-known decre-

---

[1]Not to be identified with Rolandus Bandinelli of Sienna, later Pope Alexander III. See J. NOONAN, "Who was Rolandus?," *Law, Church and Society*: Essays in

tists were Rufinus of France, later bishop of Assisi and archbishop of Sorrento († 1192), Stephanus Tornacensis, who was born in Orléans (1128) and became bishop of Tournai († 1203), Joannes Faventinus, who was born in Faenza and died there around 1187, and Albertus Beneventanus (Albertus de Mora), who became chancellor of the Roman Church in 1172 and was elected Pope as Gregory VIII on October 21, 1187 († December 17, 1187). Bologna's first *doctor utriusque iuris*, Bazianus, also composed some glosses (between 1180 and 1190). Hugo of Pisa (Huguccio), the bishop of Ferrare for twenty years (1190-1210), was the last great glossator of the *Decretum*. One of his students was Lotharius de Segni, the later Pope Innocent III (1198-1216).

In the beginning of the thirteenth century, several gloss apparatuses were composed that cannot always be clearly distinguished from the *summae*. The principal ones are those of Laurentius Hispanus and the *Glossa Palatina*, both of which were compiled between 1210 and 1215.

The most extensive textual interpretation was the *glossa ordinaria* of the decretists of the beginning of the thirteenth century.

The German Joannes Zemeca (Joannes Teutonicus), provost of Halberstadt († 1245), wrote his glossa in Bologna between 1213 and 1217 with the intention of making a practical standard apparatus that would replace all the others. He based himself principally on the apparatus of Laurentius Hispanus, the *Glossa Palatina*, the summa of Huguccio, and Roman legal texts. Bartholomaeus Brixiensis, from Brescia († 1258), supplemented it around 1245, basing himself on the collection of the *decretales* of Gregory IX. His revised edition was the model for all the later editions.

166. After the preparatory work, the decretists began to write *summae* or short, systematic expositions that they also provided with critical or exegetical commentary. Thereby, the distinction

---

*Honor of Stephan Kuttner*, Philadelphia, 1977, pp. 21-48, and R. WEIGAND, "Magister Rolandus und Papst Alexander III," *Archiv für katholisches Kirchenrecht* 149 (1980), pp. 3-44.

with the gloss apparatuses became unclear. Only Sicardus Cremonensis used the pure form of the *summa*, but he was not followed by later decretists. These often limited themselves to a few titles, so that their work was commonly called *summae titulorum*. This form was derived from the medieval Romanists. The redaction took place in two different centers, so two schools developed, that of Bologna and that of France and the Anglo-Norman islands.

The oldest *summa* of the school of Bologna is that of Paucapalea (between 1144 and 1148). The *Stroma ex decretorum corpore carptum* of magister Rolandus was found in a codex of the *Landesbibliothek* in Stuttgart. The *summa* of Rufinus, written between 1157 and 1159, may rightly be called the masterpiece of the *summae* because it was the first comprehensive work that joined the systematic method (pure *summa*) with the exegetical (*glossa*) method. It indicated a new direction that, with Huguccio, attained its zenith and end point in Bologna. It also illustrates most clearly the papal superiority in the distinction between the two powers. Stephanus Tornacensis and Joannes Faventinus also published their *summae*, around, respectively, ca. 1160 and after 1170.

Simon of Bisiniano was the first to assign a certain value to the post-Gratian decretals and so formed a bridge to the decretalists. His summa, written between March 1177 and March 1179, followed the method of Rufinus in his *summa*. Simon began with a systematic classification, which was further expanded by Sicardus of Remona. Indeed, the latter excluded from his *summa* (after 1179) all exegesis or commentary and glosses, intending only to write a systematic and didactic work. Sicardus had no successors, for Huguccio took up the previous tradition and edited between 1188 and 1191 the most extensive exegetical commentary of Gratian's work. The *Summa Reginensis*, which Queen Christina of Sweden (1626-1689) donated to the Vatican, also dates from this same period.

The *summae* of the French and Anglo-Norman school generally bear the name of a city. The *Summa Coloniensis* is the oldest: its writer, a German or French priest, limited himself to commenting on the first two parts of the decree. It originated in

Cologne in 1169-1170. Robertus Flamesburiensis wrote the *Summa Parisiensis* in Paris around 1170. In Carinthia, between 1175 and 1178, an anonymous author compiled the *Summa Monacensis*, which is now preserved in the state library in Munich. The *Summula decretalium quaestionum* (1179-1181) was written by Everardus of Ypres, a monk of Clairvaux. The *Summa Lipsiensis* was probably written in Paris or Oxford around 1186. It is called *Lipsiensis* after Leipzig, where it was found. The *Summa Bambergensis* is of French origin (1206-1210) and is in the state library in Bamberg.

167. In addition to the actual *summae*, the decretists also used other forms of explanation. In the *distinctiones* they tried to define the meaning of legal concepts. In a *casus* they treated the *species facti* and gave them a *solutio iuris*. In the margin they would also add *notabilia*, comments introduced by the word *nota* or *notandum est*. Later, these *notabilia* were compiled in separate books. Everyday teaching practice produced *quaestiones* or unresolved legal questions in which pros and cons were weighed in order to come to a definite answer. *Omnibonus*, the later bishop of Verona (1157-1185), drew up an *abbreviatio* around 1156, a selection of texts from either a part of or from the entire collection with the original division being maintained. Finally, the decretists tried several times to order the decree according to other systems in the *Transformationes Decreti*.

B) The First Decretalists

168. The first decretalists worked on the *Quinque Compilationes Antiquae*. They began with glosses and gloss apparatuses and ended with *summae*. Glosses were added primarily to the *Compilatio prima*, not only by Bernardus Papiensis himself, but also by Petrus, Laurentius, Vincentius Hispanus, and others. Tancredus of Bologna (ca. 1185 - ca. 1235) is certainly the most eminent, and is rightly called the *magister decretorum*. His wide knowledge of Roman and canon law earned him the confidence of the popes. Damasus, probably from Hungary, and professor in Bologna

from 1210 until 1220, also wrote glosses. On the British Isles, too, decretalists like Richardus and Alanus Anglicus and Joannes Gallensis were active. All of them worked on the other compilations. But the glosses by Jacob de Albenga (†1274) in the *compilatio* I were used as *glossa ordinaria*.

169. Bernardus Papiensis himself wrote the first *summa* on his *Breviarium Extravagantium*, also later known as *Compilatio I*. It was composed while Bernardus was bishop of Faenza (1191/2-1198). It was used as a textbook in the school of Bologna and by all the following decretalists. The large number of manuscripts of this work testifies to its wide distribution.

The *Summa Iuris Canonici* of Raymond of Penafort is not a decree or a *summa* of decretals but more of a handbook in seven parts. Raymond composed it according to his own method and based it on the plan of the *Decretum* and the *Compilationes*. He wrote it while he was a professor in Bologna, before he joined the Dominicans on 1 April 1222 or 1224. Damasus already had written his *Summa* before 1215.

170. Special writings also existed at this time. *Brocarda* or *generalia* were expositions that gave the results of a discussion in a concise form. From a pro and con argumentation, a legal principle was easily derived. In addition, there were *Quaestiones* and *Abbreviationes*. Special tracts were published on various legal subjects. Both Bernardus Papiensis and Tancredus wrote a *Summa de matrimonio*, the former around 1170, the latter between 1210 and 1214. Bernardus also wrote on the right to vote in his *Summa de Electione*. Finally, many *Ordines iudiciarii*, which dealt with process law, were written at the end of the twelfth and the beginning of the thirteenth century. For example, Richardus Anglicus, Damasus, and Tancredus produced such works.

171. Bibliography of the Science of Law (of A and B)

A. VAN HOVE, *o.c.*, nos. 412-426 (A), 428-436 (B), 437-450 (other writings).

J.F. von SCHULTE, *Die Geschichte der Quellen und Literatur des canonischen Rechts*, vol. I, Stuttgart, 1875 (anastatic reprint, Graz, 1956), pp. 109-239.

S. KUTTNER, *Repertorium der Kanonistik (1140-1234)*, Città del Vaticano, 1937 (anastatic reprint, Modena, 1981), pp. 125-166 (A); 322-396, 438-442 (B).

K.W. NÖRR, *Die Kanonistische Literatur*, cfr H. COING, *o.c.*, 1937, vol. I, pp. 365-375.

W.M. PLÖCHL, *o.c.*, vol. II, pp. 496-513.

G. LE BRAS - CH. LEFÈBVRE - J. RAMBAUD, Vol. VII, *L'âge classique (1140-1378), Sources et théorie du droit*, Paris, 1965, pp. 222-305.

J.A. CLARENCE SMITH, *o.c.*, nrs. 10-61.

G. FRANSEN, "Les quetsions disputées dans les facultés de droit," *Les questions disputées et les questions quodlibétiques dans les facultés de théologie, de droit et de médecine* (*Typologie des sources du moyen âge occidental*, fasc. 44-45), Turnhout, 1985, pp. 223-277.

J. RAMBAUD-BUHOT, "L'Abbreviatio Decreti d'Omnebene," *Proceedings of the Sixth International Congress of Medieval Canon Law. Berkeley. California, 28 July - 2 August 1980. Monumenta iuris canonici*, ser. C, vol. 7, Città del Vaticano, 1985, pp. 93-107.

*Miscellanea Rolando Bandinelli, Papa Alexandro III*. Studi raccolti da Filippo LIOTTA, Sienna, 1986, XX - 497 p.

172. Principal Editions

J.F. von SCHULTE, *Die Summa des Paucapalea über das Decretum Gratiani*, Giessen, 1890 (anastatic reprint, Aalen, 1965).

F. THANER, *Die Summa Magistri Rolandi*, Innsbruck, 1874 (anastatic reprint, Aalen, 1973).

H. SINGER, *Die Summa decretorum des Magister Rufinus*, Paderborn, 1902 (anastatic reprint, Aalen, 1963).

J.F. von SCHULTE, *Die Summa des Stephanus Tornacensis über das Decretum Gratiani*, Giessen, 1891 (anastatic reprint, Aalen, 1965).

G. FRANSEN - S. KUTTNER, *Summa «Elegantius in iure divino» seu Coloniensis*, 3 vols., New York, 1969 and 1978. Città del Vaticano 1986, *Monumenta iuris canonici*, ser. A, vol. 1.

T.P. MCLAUFHLIN, *The summa Parisienis on the Decretum Gratiani*, Toronto, 1952.

X. OCHOA - A. DIEZ, *S. Raymundus de Pennaforte. Summa de iure canonico*, Rome, 1975.

E. LASPEYRES, *Bernardi Papiensis summa decretalium*, Regensburg, 1860 (anastatic reprint, Graz, 1956).

F. BERGMANN, *Pillius, Tancredus, Gratia. Libri de iudiciorum ordine*, Göttingen, 1842 (anastic reprint, Aalen, 1965).

L. WAHRMUND, *Die «Summa de ordine iudiciario» des Ricardus Anglicus* (*Quellen zur Geschichte des Römisch-kanonischen Prozesses im Mittelalter*, vol. II, fasc. III), Innsbruck, 1915 (anastatic reprint, Aalen, 1962).

L. WAHRMUND, *Die «Summa de ordine iudiciario» des Magister Damasus* (*Quellen zur Geschichte* ..., vol. III, fasc. IV), Innsbruck, 1926 (anastatic reprint, Aalen, 1962).

A. GARCIA Y GARCIA (ed.), *Constitutiones Concilii quarti Lateranensis una cum commentariis glossatorum*, Città del Vaticano, 1981 (= *Monumenta iuris canonici*, ser. A: *Corpus Glossatorum*, vol. 2).

K. PENNINGTON, *Joannis Teutonici Apparatus glossarum in Compilationem tertiam*, Città del Vaticano, 1981 (= *Monumenta iuris canonici*, ser. A: *Corpus Glossatorum*, vol. 3).

C) The Decretalists

173. After Gregory IX, the primary basis for study and commentaries beside the *Decretum Gratiani*, was formed by the three authentic collections which consisted mainly of papal decretals. Therefore, their commentators are called decretalists. The *Extravagantes* are discussed less frequently.

174. In the decretals of Gregory IX, three different methods were used in turn.

Bernardus Parmensis de Bottone is the most important of the glossators, and his gloss was accepted as *glossa ordinaria*. He was born in Parma at the beginning of the thirteenth century, became a professor and a canon in Bologna, and died there in May 1263. Goffredus de Trano, named after his birthplace in Apulia, was professor of civil law in Naples and of canon law in Bologna. Somewhere before 1241 he wrote glosses on the *decretalia* of Gregory IX, and between 1241 and 1243 he made up a manual, the *Summa de rubricis Decretalium*. He became a cardinal-deacon in 1244 and died around April 1245. Petrus de Sampsona, who was born near Nîmes, taught in Bologna between 1230 and 1260. The glosses of Vincentius Hispanus, first professor in Bologna (1212-1230) and then probably bishop of Idanha-Guarda in Portugal († 1248) were quite valuable too.

Joannes Hispanus de Petesella, who became professor in Bologna in 1223 and later in Pavia, Goffredus of Trano, Bernardus Parmensis de Bottone, and Balduinus Brandeburgensis, a Franciscan, published writings with a brief systematic treatise on each of the titles, hence, the *summae titulorum*. Undoubtedly, Henricus de Segusio, who was called "Hostiensis" as cardinal of Ostia, was the most erudite. We know of his *commentaria* on the constitutions of Innocent IV, but his most important work is his *summa* rewritten between 1250-1253 after a fire had destroyed the original. Thus, it is rightly called the *summa aurea*. As a doctor of canon and civil law, Henricus has been given the title *utriusque iuris monarcha*. He died in 1271. During the Middle Ages, to study canon law was "*Hostiensem sequi*."

Finally, some wrote exegetical commentaries on each part of every chapter in *commentaria* or *lecturae*. During his pontificate, Innocent IV (1243-1254), previously called Sinibaldus Fliscus and professor in Bologna, wrote a very methodical work. Others who worked in the same manner were the Benedictine abbot of Montmajour, Bernardus de Montemirato, called Abbas Antiquus († 1296), Henricus de Segusio, and Aegidius de Fuscarariis († 1289), who, in 1252, became the first married layman to teach canon law in Bologna. Joannes Andreae (ca. 1270-1348) was, without doubt, the most important commentator. In his *Commentaria novella in Decretales Gregorii IX* (ca. 1338), he not only gave exegetical explanations but also discussed the opinions of previous commentators and resolved disputes ingeniously. Therefore, he is rightly called the *Pater et tuba iuris canonici*. His whole family was involved in the study of canon law: he discussed legal problems with his wife Melancia; his eldest son Bonencontra became a professor in canon law in Bologna and Padua; and his youngest daughter, Novella, after whom he entitled his work, assisted him in his classes.

After Ioannes, we find other great names, but they all remained in his shadow: Henricus Boich from England, a lecturer in Paris († ca. 1350), Joannes de Lignano († 1383), Aegidius de Bellamera († 1407), Petrus de Ancharano († 1416), Antonius de Butrio († 1408), a layman whose courses were attended by many and who trained renowned jurists like Franciscus Zabarella, who is sometimes called Cardinalis († 1417), and, finally, Dominicus de Sancto Geminiano († 1436).

At the end of the Middle Ages, the number of decretalists declined significantly. We only mention some of the most noteworthy of them. Francis Zabarella, a professor of Bologna, bishop of Florence, cardinal and president of the Council of Constanz (1414-1418) was well known for his *commentaria* on the *liber extra* and the *Clementinae*. Nicolaus de Tudeschis or Abbas Siculus was a Benedictine monk and abbot, born in Sicily, who died in 1445. In 1434 he became archbishop of Palermo and was therefore often called Panhormitanus. To distinguish him from Bernardus de Montemirato, *Abbas antiquus*, he is also called *Abbas modernus*. Felinus Sandaeus came from Felina in Reggio and died in 1503 in Lucca, where he was the bishop. Although Philippus Decius (1454-1536/7) sometimes used false citations to support his arguments, his commentary on the Decretals is generally praised.

175. Some writers limited their work to only a few parts of the Decretals. Baldus de Ubaldis (ca. 1319-1400), a famous jurist and canonist, taught in several Italian universities but principally in Perugia, the city of his birth. He wrote about the first three books of the Decretals, and he dealt at length with canon law in his commentary on the *Codex Iustiniani*. Joannes ab Imola († 1436) also discussed only these first three books. Antonius de Rosellis, from Arezzo, wrote exclusively on the second and third books, while Joannes Antonius de Sancto Georgio treated the fourth. He was called *praepositus* because he was initially the provost of the cathedral of Milan. He died in 1509 as a cardinal. Of Guido Papa (Guipape † 1487), a lawyer in Grenoble, only a few titles are known.

176. These methods were commonly applied in the *Liber Sextus Bonifacii VIII*. The most important *apparatus glossarum* is from the hand of Joannes Monachus († 1313), Guido de Baysio (archdeacon, † 1313), who worked in the papal curia in Avignon, and Joannes Andreae, who wrote the *glossa ordinaria*. In addition to the *doctores* who wrote *commentaria seu lecturae* on the decretals of Gregory IX, we have to mention Albericus de Rosate or Rosciate († 1354) for the *Liber Sextus*. He wrote a *dictionnarium* (ca. 1338) in which he gave the meanings of the words, taken

from both sectors of law and arranged alphabetically, with references to the authors.

Of some fame, too, were Guillielmus de Monte Lauduno, a Benedictine abbot († 1343), Philippus Franchus de Franchis from Perugia († 1471), and Ludovicus Gomesius from Spain († 1553).

There were fewer commentaries on the *Clementinae*. Only Joannes Andreae produced an *Apparatus glossarum*. The *commentaria seu lecturae* are from the hand of Guillielmus de Monte Lauduno, Mattheus Romanus (fourteenth century), Joannes Andreae and his student Paulus de Liazariis († 1356), Petrus de Ancharano, Franciscus Zabarella, and Nicolaus de Tudeschis.

D) A Wide Choice of Writings

177. The *glossae, summae*, and *commentaria* were not the only forms of critical study of the sources of canon law used in the thirteenth and fourteenth centuries. In *summaria* —also called *repertoria, breviaria, memoralia*, or *vocabularia*— the content of the collections was given in an abbreviated form. The *Notabilia*, for example, of Martinus de Fano († ca. 1375) and Joannes de Deo, who taught between 1247 and 1253, reproduced only the principal parts. In this context the value of dictionaries was revealed. These were called *Tabulae alphabeticae iuris, repertoria*, or *vocabularia*. The *dictionnarium* of Alericus de Rosate turned out to be of great practical value. To familiarize the students with the application of the various principles to concrete cases, *casus* were compiled, collections of theoretical or practical cases. Tracts on specific subjects were preferred by many authors. The *ordines iudiciarii*, for instance those of Martinus de Fano (ca. 1260) and of Aegidius de Fuscaraiis (1265) were also popular. This is evidenced in the many later editions of L. Wahrmund, *Der "Ordo Iudiciorum" des Martinus de Fano (Quellen zur Geschichte des Römisch-Kanonischen Prozesses im Mittelalter*, vol. I, Book VII), Innsbruck, 1906 (anastatic reprint, Aalen, 1962); *Der "Ordo iudiciarius" des Aegidius Fuscarariis (Quellen zur Geschichte ...*, vol. III, Book I), Innsbruck, 1916 (anastatic reprint, Aalen, 1962).

Guillielmus Durantis (1237-1296), who held various important offices in the Roman Curia, from 1280 to 1291, and who took over the episcopal see of Mende, wrote a *Speculum iudicale* around 1287. Therefore he was called *Speculator*. It was an exceptional tract on both canonical and civil procedures. In his *Repertorium aureum*, Martinus compiled questions of canon law with references to the texts that could provide solutions. Interesting, too, are the *Lectura super arboribus consanguinitatis et affinitatis*, a tract on consanguinity and affinity by Joannes Andreae and the *Commentarium super regulis iuris* by Dinus Mugellanus († 1303).

From the middle of the thirteenth century to the middle of the fifteenth century, commentaries were still produced on the *Decretum Gratiani*. The most noteworthy commentaries are those of Petrus de Salinis and Joannes de Pinthona, both from the middle of the thirteenth century, and of the already mentioned Aegidius de Bellamera, Dominicus de Sancto Geminiano, Antonius de S. Georgio, and Joannes de Turrecremata, a Spanish Dominican († 1468). The tract of Guido de Baysio is by far the most important and is known under the name of *Apparatus ad decretum* or *Rosarium* (1300).

178. Bibliography of C and D

A. VAN HOVE, *o.c.*, nos. 437-450, 453-492.
J.F. von SCHULTE, *o.c.*, vol. II, pp. 75-556, pp. 123-129 (Hostiensis), pp. 130-132 (Abbas antiquus), pp. 205-230 (Joannes Andreae), pp. 275-277 (Baldus de Ubaldis), etc.
W.M. PLÖCHL, *o.c.*, vol. II, pp. 513-527.
G. LE BRAS - C. LEFÈBVRE - J. RAMBAUD, *L'âge classique, 1140-1378*, Paris, 1965, pp. 308-337.
G. FRANSEN, "Trente ans de recherches dans les manuscrits du droit canonique classique," *L'année canonique* 12 (1968), pp. 31-47.
P. OURLIAC - H. GILLES, *La période post-classique, 1378-1500*, Paris, 1971, pp. 11-64, 87-149.
K.W. NÖRR, *Die Kanonistische Literatur*, cfr H. COING, 1973, vol. I, pp. 376-382.
J.A. CLARENCE SMITH, *o.c.*, nos. 62-167.
W. ULLMANN, *o.c.*, pp. 83-116, 163-189.

M. BERTRAM, "Kanonistische Quästionensammlungen von Bartholomäus Brixiensis bis Joannes Andreae," *Proceedings of the Seventh International Congress of Medieval Canon Law*, Cambridge, 23-27 July 1984, Città del Vaticano, 1988, pp. 265-281, (*Monumenta Iuris Canonici*, series C: subsidia, vol. 8).

K. PENNINGTON, "Joannes Andreae's Additions to the Decretals of Gregory IX," *Zeitschrift der Savigny-Stiftung für Rechtsgeschichte. Kanonistische Abteilung* 74 (1988), pp. 328-347.

E) The Study of Canon Law

179. In the thirteenth century, the study of canon law flourished again in the episcopal schools. Innocent IV founded a school for theology and canon law at the Roman Curia in 1245. Canon law was taught principally at the universities of Bologna and Padua in Italy, Toulouse, Orléans, Montpellier, and Paris in France, and Palencia (up to 1262) in Spain. In the monasteries the work proceeded more selectively. A statutory regulation of 1188 stipulated that the Cistercians could not keep the *Decretum Gratiani* in a communal cabinet because it could mislead the monks. This prohibition was renewed in 1240 and 1289. In the fourteenth century, in 1335 and 1350, it was even forbidden to teach canon law in or out of monasteries or to study it. The Dominicans extracted the texts they were interested in — on the *forum internum* and confession — from the various law books. From the *Liber Sextus* they selected the parts that dealt with the privileges of the mendicant orders. For the Franciscans, from 1292 on, theology and canon law had to be strictly distinguished and both subjects were taught in separate rooms by other professors. Benedict XII permitted the Benedictines in 1336 and the regular canons of St. Augustine in 1339 to study and to teach canon law. Nevertheless, canon law on the *forum externum* remained of secondary importance. The members of religious orders could not even study Roman law, which was inseparably linked to it. Their interest was to be confined only to theology.

For the secular clergy, the study of canon law was useful. In the diocesan curias, ecclesiastical norms had force of law, and were often applied to resolve problems, even civil problems.

Moreover, knowledge of the science of law opened the way for the secular clergy to honorable and profitable offices, benefices, and privileges. Not surprisingly, the laity, too, took up the study of canon law.

F) Interwoven with Moral Theology

180. Because of the intimate bond between law and moral theology — indeed, ethics are at the foundation of all legal systems — moralists make up rules of law. Therefore, the writings of moralists cannot be ignored as sources for the science of law. The general theological writings of theologians like Peter Lombard († 1164) and Thomas Aquinas († 1274) provide a considerable amount of information about legal institutions and their evolution. Works of medieval moral theologians, for example, St. Anthoninus (1389-1459), who was bishop of Florence, are of great importance. Sometimes specific subjects are treated, such as trade, contracts, and money, in which law is assigned an even more important role than moral theology.

The *Summae confessorum, summae casuum* or *de casibus conscientiae*, constitute a successor to the *libri paenitentiales*, after the example of the *paenitentiale* (1208-1215) of Robertus Flamesburiensis. They contain rules of law concerned exclusively with auricular or private confession. This became popular after the Fourth Lateran Council (1215) legally imposed annual confession. In 1216, the *Summa confessorum* of Thomas of Chobham spread throughout England. This work was written specifically for the use of the English clergy. F. BROOMFIELD published it in the *Analecta Mediaevalia Namurcensia*, vol. 25 (1968).

The thirteenth century also saw the *Compilatio praesens*, a "*summa de confessione*" from around 1220 by Petrus Pictavensis (Pierre de Poitiers), which has been published in the *Corpus Christianorum, continuatio mediaevalis* 50 (1980) by J. Longère. Of considerable influence, too, was the *summa casuum*, also known as the *summa de paenitentia* or *summa de casibus conscientiae* by Raymundus de Pennaforte. It consisted of three books, composed in Barcelona between 1224 and 1226. After the *Liber*

*Extra*, a second version appeared somewhere between 1234 and 1236. Because of the fact that the confessors were often confronted with matrimonial matters during confession, Raymundus had been asked to write a *summa de matrimonio* (1235-1236). This appeared to be a revision of Tancredus' *summa*, a collection put together between 1210 and 1214. Although it was distinct from the *summa de paenitentia*, many of the manuscripts added it to the latter as a sort of continuation or fourth book. The *Summa Monaldina* or the *Summa de Iure tractans* (before 1274) of Monaldus, the *Summa Joannina* (ca. 1290) of Joannes Friburgensis, which completed the *Summa Raymundiana*, and the *Summa confessorum* (end thirteenth century) of Joannes Erfordiensis, called Joannes de Saxonia, were published during this time.

An important fourteenth century work is the *Summa Astesana* (1317). It was written by the Franciscan Astesanus in the style of the Franciscan school of theology (John Duns Scotus). In this respect, it differed considerably from the *summae*, which were written by Dominicans. The *Summa rudium* (ca. 1336) ("*ad utilitatem et ad informationem simplicium et minus peritorum sacerdotum*"), which was composed by an anonymous German Dominican for priests on the basis of the *Summa Joannina*, and the *Summa Pisana* or *Pisanella* (before 1338) by Bartholomaeus a S. Concordio date from the first half of the fourteenth century.

Noteworthy also is the *Summa pauperum* or *Summula de Summa*, an abbreviated edition of the *Summa Raymundiana*. It was written in the middle of the fourteenth century by Adam Teutonicus, probably a Cistercian monk from the Abbey of Aldersbach near Passau in Bavaria.

The *Summa Angelica* (ca. 1486), the *Summa Baptistiniana* or *Rosella* (end of the fifteenth century), the *Summa Tabiena* (1515), and the *Summa Sylvestrina* or *Summa Summarum* (beginning of the sixteenth century) were written by, respectively, Angelus Carletus de Clavasio, Joannes Baptista de Salis or Trovamala, Joannes de Tabia, and Sylvester Prierias.

Editions

X. Ochoa - A. Diez, *S. Raimundus de Pennaforte Summa de paenitentia*, Rome, 1976 (*Universa bibliotheca iuris*, vol. I, fasc. B.).
Id., *S. Raimundus de Pennaforte, Summa de matrimonio*, Rome, 1978 (*Universa bibliotheca iuris*, vol. I, fasc. C).

Bibliography

J.G. Ziegler, *Die Ehelehre des Pönitentialsummen von 1200-1350*, Regensburg, 1956.
P. Michaud - Quantin, *Sommes de casuistique et manuels de confession au moyen-âge (XII-XIV siècles)*, Louvain-Lille-Montreal, 1962, (*Analecta mediaevalia Namurcensia*, N° 13).

G) The Influence of Roman Law

181. The *Ius Romanum Iustinianeum* was also important as *ius suppletivum* and *confirmatorium*, since it was largely inspired by a Christian spirit and based on *aequitas* and *humanitas*. The medieval canonists supplemented canon law with rules from Roman law, which they adapted and corrected in a Christian sense. In case of gaps or doubts, the Justinian law served as *ius suppletorium* and *confirmatorium*.

Many jurists of that time were trained in both canon and civil law. The schools of civil and canon law often maintained close relationships with each other and sometimes even formed one faculty, the *utriusque iuris*.

From the eighth century on, the influence of Roman law gradually declined almost to the point of disappearance in the tenth and eleventh centuries. With the general intellectual revival in Italy around 1100, the study of Roman law revived in Bologna.

182. In this period Irnerius, a scholar of Bologna, discovered a manuscript of the Digests and with it instilled new life into the school of Bologna. He reintroduced the gloss-method. Therefore, he is considered to be at the basis of the school of the glossators. Among his pupils are the *quattuor doctores*: Bulgarus, Martinus Gosia, Jacobus, and Ugo de Porta Ravennate, all from the

twelfth century. They studied Roman Law as a coherent legal system in itself, independent of the law of their time.

In the thirteenth century, Azo (ca. 1150-1230) and his student Accursius (ca. 1182-1263) occupied the chair of Irnerius. The *glossa Accursii* was often consulted in legal practice. As the *glossa ordinaria* up to 1627, it was often printed in the margin or interlinearly in the *Corpus Iuris Civilis*, which was therefore called the *Corpus Iuris Civilis Glossatum*.

In these works, the glosses were treated as sources of law because they were assigned force of law by jurists: "Quidquid non agnoscit glossa, non agnoscit Curia."[1]

183. While Bologna revered the *glossa ordinaria* of Accursius, even to the point of giving it precedence over Roman Law, Padua permitted a cautious practical adaptation to the circumstances of the time. Orléans took an entirely different direction. It was very critical of the glossa of Accursius and studied Roman Law in the light of practical adaptation. Founded with the permission of Gregory IX, after Pope Honorius III had prohibited the study of Roman Law in Paris in 1219, all members of the university of Orléans were clerics. Jacques de Révigny (Ravanis, ca. 1235-1296), bishop of Verdun, and Pierre de Belleperche (Bellapertica, ca. 1250-1308), bishop of Auxerre and chancellor of France under Philip le Bel, wrote *lecturae* and *repetitiones*. Other well-known pupils of the school of Orléans were Guillielmus de Cuneo (Cunk) († 1335), professor in Toulouse and later bishop of Comminges, and Joannes Faber (Jean Faure) († ca. 1340), professor in Montpellier.

184. In the fourteenth century, the Italian universities of Bologna, Pavia, Padua, Pisa, and Perugia were centers of the scientific study of law. Under the influence of the scholastic and dialectic methods that were used by philosophers and theolo-

---

[1] For the proceedings of the conference held in Bologna on the occasion of the seven hundredth anniversary of Accursius death, see: *Atti del convegno internazionale di studi Accursiani*, Milano, 1968, 3 vols., cxlviii-1437 p. For the works of Azo and Accursius see the *Corpus glossatorum iuris civilis*, Turino, 1966.

gians, the Italian jurists began to write long commentaries on the entire Corpus. They did not produce glosses or *summae* with long, exegetical explanations of the legal texts, but envisioned the creation of a legal system by applying the legal concepts of their time.

The Orléans method was taken over by Cynus Pistoriensis (Pistoia, 1270-1336), a student of Jacobus de Ravanis and professor in Bologna, and by Rainerius de Forlivio († 1358) of the school of Orléans. The central figure is Bartolus de Saxoferrato (1314-1357), a student of Rainerius and professor in Perugia and Pisa. In addition to extensive commentaries on almost all parts of the *Corpus Iuris Civilis*, he wrote many *consilia, quaestiones*, and tracts on private, penal, and process law. In his work, he adapted the law to the new circumstances although he never lost sight of the *glossa ordinaria* of Accursius. His work is a compromise between the methods of the earlier Italian glossators and those of the French school of Orléans.[1]

185. The students of Bartolus were called Bartolists or postglossators. Indeed, Bartolus enjoyed such great respect that it was even said that "nemo iurista nisi sit Bartolista." The most famous of his pupils is undoubtedly Baldus de Ubaldis (ca. 1319-1400), who wrote a commentary on the code of Justinian. Other pupils were: Angelus de Ubaldus († ca. 1400), Bartholomaeus a Saliceto († 1412), Joannes ab Imola († 1436), Ludovicus Pontanus Romanus († 1439), Paulus de Castro († 1441), Angelus Aretinus de Gambellionibus († after 1451), Alexander Tartagnus († 1475), Rochus Curtius († 1495), Jason de Mayno († 1519), Philippus Decius († 1536), and Andreas Tiraquellus († 1559).

186. Around 1500, the French humanists reacted to the method, language, and style of the Bartolists. They accused them of "misusing" Roman Law. As Romanists, they considered Roman

---

[1] For the proceedings of the conference held in Perugia in 1959 to commemorate his death in 1359 see: *Bartolo de Sassoferrato. Studi e documenti per il VI centenario*, 2 vols., Milano, 1962, liii-474 and 786 p. (Università degli studi di Perugia).

Law as an historical monument and refused to apply it in "modern" law. They were not at all satisfied with the reworked law from the *Codex Iuris Civilis* of Justinian. Therefore they reintroduced pre-Justinian sources. They studied the original texts from a historical or philological point of view. The basis of the humanistic, historical, or French school was the French Guillaume Budé (Budaeus, 1468-1540), philosopher, hellenist, and cofounder of the *Collège des lecteurs royaux* in 1530 in Paris, the name of which was changed to *Collège de France* after the Restoration. In 1508, he published his *Annotationes in XXIV libros Pandectarum*. The *Consilia* of Ulrich Zäsy (Zasius, 1461-1535) enjoyed some fame. The Italian Andreas Alciatus (1492-1550) and the professors Gabriël Van der Muyden (Mudaeus, 1500-1560) and Jacobus Reyvaert (1535-1568), who taught Roman Law at the universities of Louvain and Douai, followed in the humanistic tradition.

The most famous and greatest representative of the humanistic school of the science of Roman law is undoubtedly Jacobus Cujas (Cuiacius, 1522-1590) of Toulouse. He was professor at various universities, including Bourges and Valence. His works, which were published several times as *opera omnia*, witness to his great zeal. His most famous writing is certainly his twenty-eight book work, the *Observationes et Emendationes*. For canon law, we mention his *Recitationes ad Decretalium Gregorii IX libros II, III, IV* (Frankfurt, 1595). His compatriot, Hugues Doneau (Hugo Donellus, 1527-1591), also professor at various universities such as Orléans and Bourges, strived in his *Commentarium iuris civilis* to achieve a more methodical and systematic treatment of the rules of Roman law.

Dionysius Gothofredus (Denis Godefroy), who was born in Paris in 1549 and died in 1622, published the entire legislation of Justinian, in Lyons in 1583. He entitled it the *Corpus iuris civilis cum notis*, following the canonical collection that was already popularly known as the *Corpus iuris canonici*. His work was reprinted several times and used in universities and tribunals for more than a century.

The study of Roman Law was not always simply a matter of choice, however. In 1163 at the Council of Tours, Alexander III, under threat of excommunication, forbade the members of the orders to leave their monasteries for longer than two months to study law or physics. Honorius III expanded this prohibition in 1219 to archdeacons, deans, cantors, and priests, with the intention of promoting the study of theology. Often, however, dispensations were granted and special privileges awarded.

187. The period from 1140 to 1378 is called a "classical" period of canon law. After Joannes Andreae († 1348), jurisprudence began to stagnate. The jurists of the second half of the fourteenth century restricted themselves largely to compilations of existing law. This trend continued during the post-classical period, from 1378 to the beginning of the Council of Trent (1545-1563). Canon law made few advances because of a variety of external and internal factors. Rome was continually confronted with political difficulties. The exile of the popes in Avignon (1305-1378) crippled their influence. In 1378, the Church was divided by the rivalry between the pope of Rome and the pope of Avignon (Western Schism, 1378-1417), which had an obvious effect in all countries, dioceses, and parishes. This was also the reason why papal decretals were not promulgated in that time.

THIRD PERIOD
# FROM THE COUNCIL OF TRENT TO THE *CODEX IURIS CANONICI* (1917)

CHAPTER I

## FOUNDATIONS OF THE DEVELOPMENT OF CANON LAW

188. In the beginning of the sixteenth century, the general situation of the Catholic Church had reached such a low point that a total reform proved to be inevitable. The Council of Trent (1545-1563) did not confine itself to doctrinal decrees alone, but promulgated disciplinary rules also. This caused a true reform of the Church. The *decreta disciplinaria* or *decreta de reformatione* were further explained in important "appendices", such as *de matrimonio* and *de regularibus et monialibus*. The disciplinary rules were promulgated under Pius IV, in the *bulla, Benedictus Deus* of 26 January 1564. Their implementation was, to a large extent, entrusted to the diocesan bishops.

Thus, the ancient values of the Catholic Church were reestablished: the accumulation of benefices was forbidden, the residential obligation of the bishops was again taken seriously, and the pope assumed responsibility for their selection and appointment. Candidates were not eligible until the age of thirty. Every five years, each resident bishop had to make a visit *ad limina*, which Sixtus V made obligatory in 1585. Each bishop would report to the pope, orally and in writing, on the state of his diocese.

In order to have competent, resident priests, bishops required of their candidates for the priesthood a *titulus patrimonii* or a *titulus beneficii*. They had to be trained in a seminary, and each diocese had to have such a seminary. The local bishop alone had the right to admit candidates to the priesthood; *litterae testimo-*

*niales* became necessary for ordination, and the *concursus* was made obligatory for appointment as pastor. The bishops had to review all the proposed candidates, in spite of all the privileges of exemptions of abbeys, chapters, or laity.

Clear directives were given to the parish priests. They, too, had to reside in their parish and were obliged to wear the soutane under penalty of suspension or even removal from their benefice. Funeral fees were regulated; baptisms and marriages had to be registered; the impediments to marriage were clearly stipulated, such as *cognatio spiritualis, publica honestas*, and *affinitas*. Form was required for the validity of the marriage.

As a contribution to the great reform process, Pope Pius V published the *Catechismus Romanus* (1566), the *Breviarium Romanum* (1568), and the revised *Missale Romanum* (1570), as proposed by the Council.

The canons of the chapters were subject to restrictions too. Their presence in the chapter was made obligatory, the profitable practice of collation of benefices was prohibited and punished, and the bishop was given general supervision over their actions in spite of their previously acquired exemptions.

Finally, the Council also regulated monastic life, primarily by placing it under the supervision of the local bishop. New monasteries could not be founded without the permission of the bishop, and regular clergy had to obey the statutory regulations of the diocese. The monastic enclosure had to be reinstated, and the superiors — general, provincial, and local — were to be elected by secret ballot. Nuns had to be at least sixteen years old at profession. The novitiate had to be at least a year. Each new member had to bring a contribution, draw up a will, and state in writing that he or she had entered voluntarily.

189. The Council of Trent was, above all, a council of bishops. Although their obligations were more clearly stipulated and more extensive, their rights were no less important. Through the extension of the parochial visitations, the power of the individual bishop was reinforced and expanded. The Council developed

regulations concerning religious places, the clergy, the liturgy, temporal goods, religious and pious communities, and the spiritual and moral condition of the Church in the West.

The Council very persuasively confirmed the authority of the individual bishop as a delegate of the Pope. The Caesaropapal tendencies of the secular authority and the power of the exempt orders and chapters were inhibited.

190. Bibliography

N. COULET, "Les visites pastorales," *Typologie des sources du moyen âge occidental*, fasc. 23, Turnhout, 1977, 86 p. (revised edition, 1985).
H. JEDIN, *Geschichte des Konzils von Trent*, 5 vols., Freiburg, 1970-1978.
J. LECLER - H. HOLSTEIN - P. ANDÈS - C. LEFÈBVRE, *Histoire des conciles œcuméniques*, vol. XI: *Trente*, Paris, 1981.

191. The entire reform movement had a very favorable influence on the development of monastic life. The old communities revived through the merger of abbeys into congregations with the same rule and by means of strong reforms. In Spain, St. Theresa of Avila (1515-1582) carried out a reform of the Carmelites in 1562. Together with St. John of the Cross (1542-1591), she laid the foundations for the Discalced Carmelites (*Ordo Fratrum Carmelitarum Discalceatorum*, 1567). For the order, she adopted the rule of 1247 without permitting any deviations.

It was also in this period that the stricter Discalced Trinitarians and the Discalced Servite Hermits were founded. For the Cistercians, the reform of Abbot Armand Jean de Bouthillier de Rancé (1626-1700) in the monastery of La Trappe has been of permanent significance. He founded the Trappists, observing the original rule of Cîteaux: rigid silence, fasting, manual labor, and choral prayer. We find important new foundations after the French Revolution, in 1891, when Pope Leo XIII approved the rule of the *Ordo Cisterciensium Reformatorum*. Its headquarters remained at Notre-Dame de Cîteaux par Nuits-Saint-Georges in France. The women's community of the order was established already under de Rancé.

It was an active period for the traditional orders, too, such as the Dominicans, the Franciscans, (Friars Minor, Conventuals, and Capuchins), and the Carthusians.

192. A number of new orders were founded, first in Italy and Spain and later in France. These were mostly institutes of regular clergy with solemn vows who did not, however, live according to monastic rules. They were involved in quite different forms of the apostolate.

The Theatines (*Ordo Clericorum Regularium* or *Theatinorum*) were founded in 1524 in Rome by Cajetanus Thiene (1480-1547) and Petrus Caraffa (1476-1559), Bishop of Chieti (in Latin, Theate), who became Pope Paul IV. Their object was to revive religious life by means of preaching and confessing.

The Congregation of the Barnabites (*Congregatio Clericorum Regularium S. Pauli*) was founded in Milan in 1530 by Antonius Maria Zaccaria (1502-1539) and his companions. The congregation was approved in 1533 by Clement VII and set out to teach youth and to convert heretics. Its popular name was taken from the Church of St. Barnabas in Milan, where its members had served since 1545.

In 1582, St. Camillus de Lellis (1550-1614) founded a community, without vows, composed of brothers for the physical care and priests for the spiritual care of the severely ill and the dying. The Society of Camillians was raised to an order by Gregory XIV in 1591 (*Ordo Clericorum Regularium Ministrantium Infirmis*).

The most important foundation of this period is undoubtedly the *Societas Jesu* or the Jesuits, which was founded by the Spaniard Ignatius of Loyola (1491-1556) and approved by Paul III in 1540. Its objective was to defend and promote the faith. To this end, the Jesuits had permission to preach in public, organize schools, and administer the sacraments.

193. Societies with communal life but without vows were also founded. Comparable to the religious orders, these devoted themselves to the pastoral care of the people as well as nursing and the care of the sick and poor. The oldest example of such a society is

that of the Oratorians. It was founded in Rome in 1552 by Philip Neri (1515-1595) and was recognized by Gregory XIII in 1575. It was named the *Institutum (Congregatio) Oratorii S. Philippi Nerii* and devoted itself primarily to the reform of pastoral care. Inspired by the Italian society of priests of Philip Neri but totally independent, the French Oratorians (*Oratoire de France, Congregatio Oratorii Jesu et Mariae Immaculatae*) were founded in 1611 by Cardinal Pierre de Bérulle (1575-1629). They devoted themselves largely to the training of the young clergy.

A congregation more devoted to the common people was the *Congregatio Missionis* (1625) of Vincent de Paul (1581-1660), which was approved by Urban VIII in 1632. Its members, the Vincentians, were also called Lazarists after the name of their motherhouse, Saint-Lazare in Paris, where they moved in 1632. Their initial purpose was the evangelization of the poor outside the cities but they took on other tasks as well. They extended their activities to the preaching of parish missions, the administration of and teaching in seminaries, social work, and service in the foreign missions.

At the end of 1641, Jean-Jacques Olier (1608-1657) founded a seminary in Vaugirard near Paris. This was a response to the need for training of the clergy. After it was transferred in 1642 to the Parish of St. Sulpice in Paris, it became the model for all the other training centers. However, it was not Olier's intention to found the *Compagnie des prêtres de Saint-Sulpice* or the Sulpicians. The Society was approved by the Pope in 1664.

Another important congregation is that of Jesus and Mary (*Congregatio Jesu et Mariae*), better known under the name of Eudists (1643) from their founder John Eudes (1601-1680). They were primarily active in seminaries and in parish missions.

Many religious orders for women were also founded in this period. In 1544, Paul III approved the association that was dedicated to St. Ursula and thus called the Ursulines. It was founded in 1535 by Angela Merici (1474-1540) in Brescia to care for the sick and to teach young girls.

The Visitandines were founded in 1610 in Annecy under the inspiration of Francis de Sales (1567-1622) and Jeanne de Chantal (1572-1641). In 1618, the congregation was raised to an order with a monastery. In 1639, the sisters shifted their working area. Instead of caring for the sick, they henceforth devoted themselves to teaching. Undoubtedly their most famous member is St. Margaret Mary Alacoque (1647-1690) of Paray-le-Monial.

Finally, we must not forget to mention the Daughters of Charity, who undertook the care of the poor and the sick. Inspired by Vincent de Paul and Louise de Marillac (her deceased husband was named Le Gras) (1591-1660), the statutes of the congregation, founded in 1663, were approved in 1668 by Pope Clement XI.

Bibliography

R. LEMOINE, "Le monde des religieux," *Histoire du droit et des institutions d'Église en Occident*, vol. XV, part 2: *L'époque moderne (1563-1789)*, Paris, 1976.

194.  In the sixteenth century, considerable changes were made in the papal curia. Initially, papal power was exercised by the *Presbyterium Romanum* and later by the consistory of all the cardinals. In the sixteenth century however, it became necessary to establish specialized commissions, composed of cardinals.

With the constitution *Licet ab initio* in 1542, Pope Paul III established the terrifying and misused *Congregatio Sanctae Inquisitionis haereticae pravitatis*, which was intended to guard the purity of the Catholic faith. With the reform of the Roman Curia in 1908 by Pius X, it was given the name *Sacra Congregatio Romana et Universalis Inquisitionis seu Sancti Officii* (the Holy Office) and its authority was defined more clearly.

By the Motu proprio *Alias Nos* (2 August 1564) of Pius IV, the *Sacra Congregatio Cardinalium Concilii Tridentini interpretum* received the authority to supervise the interpretation, implementation, and observance of the decrees of the Council of Trent. For this purpose, it could even issue regulations which made proper application possible. Sixtus V extended its task to the decrees of provincial and diocesan councils. Thus, it had direct supervision over the *visitationes ad limina* of the bishops, which had been made obligatory in 1585 by Sixtus V, and it supervised everything that concerned the discipline of the secular clergy and the faithful. Obviously, it was primarily this institute that was the source of post-Tridentine law and of the evolution of the *Ius Decretalium*.

In 1571, Pius V founded the *Congregatio Indicis librorum prohibitorum* and gave it the power of censorship, which Paul III had already given to the Inquisition. Only under Benedict XV this congregation lost its independence, as its task was then taken over by the Holy Office. The most obvious manifestation of its activity was the publication of the *Index librorum prohibitorum*, the official authentic collection of forbidden books, which appeared regularly after 1575.

The *Congregatio de religiosis* (°1908), which has been called the *Congregatio de religiosis et institutis saecularibus* since 1967, also originated in the sixteenth century. It was founded in 1572 by Pope Pius V as the *Congregatio super consultationibus episcoporum et aliorum praelatorum*. Sixtus V added to it the *Congregatio pro consultationibus regularium* in 1586. The two were combined into one body in 1601 by Clement VIII.

With the constitution *Immensa Dei* of 22 January 1588, Sixtus V founded the *Congregatio pro sacris ritibus et caeremoniis* to supervise the reform of ceremonies, rites, and liturgical books. It had authority over canonization and beatification, the reception of princes and eminent people in Rome, and questions of protocol. At the same time, the *Congregatio pro erectione ecclesiarum et provisionibus consistorialibus* was founded. Later on it was called the *Congregatio consistorialis* and, since 1967, the *Congregatio pro episcopis*. Its primary task was the preparation of the *causae majores*, which had to be dealt with in the secret consistory. It was also responsible for the establishment, division, and abolition of dioceses, and the appointment of bishops.

The same constitution established the *Congregatio caeremonialis*. Its authority extended only to the liturgical ceremonies of popes and cardinals, the civil ceremonies of the papal palace involving members of the Holy See and of other states, and the solution of juridical problems arising in this area.

After attempts by Pius V in 1568, Gregory XIII in 1576, and Clement VIII in 1599, who established commissions of cardinals to defend and expand the faith, Gregory XV founded the *Congregatio de Propaganda Fide* by means of the constitution *Inscrutabili divinae Providentiae* of 22 June 1622. It had ultimate authority over the missions.

The activities of these congregations and of those founded later became important sources of new law. They created the *praxis* and the *stylus* of the *Curia Romana* and thus formed a new source of canon law.

195. The supreme judicial power is exercised by the Holy See through three tribunals: the *Rota Romana* and the *Signatura Apostolica* deal with disputes in the *external forum*; the Sacred Penitentiary has authority over the *internal forum*.

The Roman Rota is without any doubt the most important. During the twelfth century, its size was increased because it was consulted so often and because the juridical activity of the Pope had increased substantially. From the fourteenth to the eighteenth century, its authority extended over a wide range of subjects. It dealt with *causae beneficiales, jurisdictionis, matrimoniales, super nullitate professionis*, exemptions, and patronal rights. Even today, it is the most active court of the universal church.

The jurisprudence of the Pope is easily recognizable in the *Signatura Apostolica*. Petitions and disputes presented to the Pope are handled here by his delegates. In the sixteenth century, this institute was divided into two departments, the *Signatura Gratiae* and the *Signatura Iustitiae*, which dealt, respectively, with administrative and judicial matters.

The earliest writings that mention *paenitentiarii papales*, who were priests acting in the name of the Pope who granted forgiveness of sins and removal of censures, date from the twelfth century. In the thirteenth century, these priests formed a college with a cardinal at its head. Their jurisdiction extended initially to both the external forum and the internal forum. Their authority was defined by Benedict XII in 1338.

196. Finally, we have to mention the papal administration, which contributed in no small measure to the development of canon law under the form of the Apostolic Chancellary, the Apostolic Datary, the Apostolic Chamber, the Secretariat of State, and the Secretariat of the briefs.

Bibliography

W.M. PLÖCHL, *o.c.*, vol. III, pp. 144-182.
P. ANDRIEU - GUITRANCOURT, *o.c.,* pp. 815-846.

197. In addition to the evolution within the Church, external factors must not be overlooked. Undoubtedly, Protestantism, Gallicanism, Episcopalism, Josephism, and the *schola iuris naturalis* left their mark on the direction taken by Church and are at the foundation of what the Church and its law are today.

## Chapter II
## DOCUMENTARY SOURCES

198. Popes, councils, and the Roman Curia produced a flood of norms and regulations. However, they were systematically organized in numerous compilations, which was inconvenient for historical purposes. At the time of the Council of Trent, there was a tendency to collect the acts more or less chronologically. For instance, the reform of the liturgy is stipulated in the prescriptions of the post-Tridentine popes. Nevertheless, a number of canonists still tried to order Church laws in a systematic fashion.

We will give a short overview of the collections of papal acts, of councils, and of the Roman Curia (A 1-3), of the new liturgical books (B), and also of the attempts to compile authentic collections (C).

A) Collections of Acts of Popes, Councils, and the Roman Curia.

199. After the Council of Trent, legislation was made primarily by the Pope, and by the Roman Dicasteries in his name. From the second half of the sixteenth century onwards, legal scholars had recourse to chronological collections, to which they added documents of earlier periods. Because of the criticism and zeal of opponents of the Catholic doctrine, canonists were forced to find the original texts. In the original, unchanged redactions, they tried to find the foundations of the Catholic faith. The medieval jurists had adapted these texts in order to explain and actualize the will of the legislator. For this same reason, the preference was given to a chronological order with a systematic index.

## 1) Collections of Papal Acts

200. The Church is administered primarily through written regulations. The papal acts are an important source of canon law. According to Pope Liberius (352-366) in his *Epistula Uniformis*, the papal acts, in their entirety or in summary, were registered and carefully preserved in the archives of the papal chancellery during the middle of the fourth century. The documents were compiled by the Roman Curia in registers. Almost all of them up to Innocent III (1198-1216) have been lost, although references or citations are present in canonical collections, particularly in the *Corpus Iuris Canonici*. In the sixteenth century, they were again compiled chronologically in the *bullaria* in order to facilitate refutation of the protests and objections of the Reformers.

The *bullaria particularia*, as distinct from the *bullaria generalia*, include acts that are concerned with particular places (countries and dioceses), persons (e.g., religious orders), or objects (e.g., privileges, monastic rules, patronal rights).

201. The *Bullarium* of Laertius Cherubini († 1626) contains 922 acts from Gregory VII (1078-1085) to Sixtus V (1585-1590). It was published in 1586 in Rome in three volumes and forms the basis for subsequent collections. Laertius Cherubini was the first to use the term *bullarium*. He collected the later acts (115) of Sixtus V in 1588 and 1590 in supplements, and in 1617 he published an enlarged edition in three volumes with 732 new acts. His son, Angelus Maria Cherubini, a Benedictine, collected the acts of Paul V (1605-1621), Gregory XV (1621-1623), and Urban VIII (1623-1644) in a fourth volume (1633). In 1638, he made up a third, enlarged edition in four volumes with acts from 440 (Leo the Great) to 1637 (Urban VIII).

The Franciscans, Angelus a Lantusca and Joannes Paulus a Roma, completed the *bullarium* in 1672 with two volumes consisting of the remaining acts of Urban VIII and the first three years of Clement X (1670-1676). In 1673, a new edition in six volumes with an appendix appeared in Rome and another, in five volumes without appendix, in Lyons.

202. Hieronymus Mainardi published a seventh volume in the series of the *Bullarium Cherubini* in 1733 in Rome under the title *Bullarium Romanum*. It contains the acts of Clement X. He also added another seven volumes with the papal acts up to 1740 (Clement XII) (Rome, 1734-1744). In almost the same period, namely from 1739 to 1762, Carolus Cocquelines († 1758), an assistant of Mainardi, put together a new edition of the six volumes of the *Bullarium Cherubini*. He added acts from 440 (Leo the Great) to 1669 (Clement IX) so that the new edition consisted of twenty volumes in six parts. Mainardi completed it with the *Bullarium Benedicti XIV*.

The *Magnum Bullarium Romanum* (Mainardi-Cocquelines) thus consisted of eighteen parts in thirty-two volumes with acts from 440 to 1758, namely, the six parts of Cherubini extended by C. Cocquelines to twenty volumes with acts from 440 to 1669, followed by the eight parts (volumes) of H. Mainardi with acts from 1670 to 1740, and concluded by four parts (volumes) from Benedict XIV (1740-1758). The compilation of the entire *Bullarium* took over thirty years from 1733 until 1762. An anastatic reprint of thirty-two parts in thirteen volumes of the Roman edition (1733-1762) by H. Mainardi and C. Cocquelines appeared in Graz in 1964-1967. Because of its size, the *Bullarium* of Mainardi overshadowed that of Cherubini and claimed the exclusive title of *Bullarium Romanum*.

The *Magnum Bullarium Romanum* was supplemented, first with acts from 1758 to 1834 in nineteen parts, fourteen volumes, and one fascicule (Rome 1835-1837) and then with acts from 1758 to 1830 in ten volumes (Prato, 1840-1856). An anastatic reprint of the *Continuatio* (Rome, 1835-1857; nineteen parts in nine volumes) was published in Graz in 1963-1964.

203. Around the time of the appearance of the Mainardi-Cocquelines work, Andreas Chevalier published another bullarium: the *Bullarium Luxemburgense*. Although the title indicates that it was published in Luxemburg, it was in fact published in Geneva. The first edition of 1727 had eight volumes, with another

eleven volumes up to 1758. Chevalier derived his material largely from acts of Mainardi-Cocquelines. The entire set of nineteen volumes covers the period from 440 to 1758. A new edition of the *Magnum Bullarium Romanum* was published between 1857 and 1872 and named the *Bullarium Taurinense* after Turin, where it was published. It contains twenty-four parts from 440 to 1740. Two appendices completed it. The first was published in 1867 and contains acts from 440 to 536 (Pope Sylverius); the second was intended to contain five volumes, i.e., the four volumes of Benedict XIV, now chronologically ordered, and a fifth with about three-hundred acts from the same Pope in first edition. Only the last volume was published in Naples in 1885.

The Luxemburg and the Turin *bullarium* were also given the name *bullarium Romanum*. This title came to be reserved for the *bullarium* of Mainardi-Cocquelines.

204. Acts of more recent date, those from after 1834 or after the *Bullarium Romanum* with its supplements, are contained in the separate editions of the acts of Gregory XVI (1831-1846) in four volumes, Pius IX (1846-1878) in nine volumes, Leo XIII (1878-1905) in twenty-three volumes, and Pius X (1905-1914) to 1908 in five volumes.

For the period from 1908 to 1965, the most important acts of the popes and the Roman dicasteries have been compiled in the *Acta Sanctae Sedis* (forty-one volumes). Up to the official declaration of 23 May 1904 by Pius X, they remain private in nature. Since 1909, the *Acta Apostolicae Sedis* have been the official commentary of the Holy See.

205. In addition to the general *bullaria*, there are also the particular *bullaria*, which contain the acts concerning persons, countries or regions, objects, and particular eras. Beginning in the eighteenth century, many scholars compiled critical editions of these acts. Strictly speaking, we may call them *bullaria*, but they have their own character because of their critical approach.[1]

---

[1] For the innumerable editions, we refer to A. Stickler, *op. cit.*, pp. 303-318; J. Gaudemet, "Droit canonique," *Introduction bibliographique à l'histoire et l'éthno-*

## 2) Collections of Conciliar Documents

206. The acts of the various councils have been compiled in a similar way. The ecumenical councils, twenty-one in all, bring together the entire Catholic Church. After the Council of Trent, which is certainly the most important, only Vatican I (1869-1870) and Vatican II (1962-1965) have taken place. The particular councils are numerous. The *concilia provincialia* group all bishops in one ecclesiastical province under the chairmanship of the metropolitan. According to the stipulations of the Council of Trent, they must be held every three years. The *concilia dioecesana* or synods are much less frequent, even though Trent had prescribed that they be convened annually. In the nineteenth century, *concilia nationalia vel plenaria* were held under the chairmanship of a papal legate.

The conciliar canons were written down in one of three ways. The *collectiones singulares* contained only acts of the individual councils; the *collectiones particulares* concerned a particular region, era, or subject; and the *collectiones generales (relative)* attempted to include the specifications of all previous councils, both particular and ecumenical.

207. The first general collections arose, as did the Council of Trent, from the reaction against Protestantism.

Jacobus Merlin (ca. 1480-1541) published his two-volume work in Paris in 1524, 1530, and 1535. It contains documents of the first six ecumenical councils, of the two reformist councils, Constance (1414-1418) and Basel (1431-1443), and of forty-seven provincial councils, as well as sixty-nine papal decrees.

Petrus Crabbe (1471572-1544), a Franciscan, published his collection of general and particular councils in two volumes in

---

*logie juridique*, B/9, Paris, 1963, pp. 26-36. For the acts of the popes, see: *Patrologia Latina* of J.P. Migne, the *Monumenta Germaniae Historica*, both in their *Sectio Epistolarum* and in their *Epistolae saec. XIII e registris RR. Pontificum selectae*, and the publications in the series *Bibliothèque des Écoles françaises d'Athènes et de Rome* (Paris).

A short summary and analysis can be found in the series of works mentioned above by Jaffé and Potthats, S. Loewenfeld, and J. von Pflugh-Harttung.

Cologne in 1538. A second edition in three volumes followed in 1551.

Starting with the acts of the Council of Trent, publication became part of the procedure. Petrus Crabbe was followed by individuals such as Laurentius Surius (1522-1578), a Carthusian (four volumes, Cologne, 1567); Dominicus Bollanus, a Dominican, who had his five volumes published in Venice in 1587 by Dominicus Nicolini; Severinus Binius (1573-1641), a professor in Cologne (four parts, five volumes, Cologne, 1606[1]; four parts, nine volumes, Cologne, 1618[2]; nine parts, eleven volumes, Paris, 1636[3]); and a group of canonists who completed the *Collectio Romana* in four parts in Rome between 1608 and 1612. Paul V called it *Romana*.

208. During the second half of the seventeenth century, a number of even more important collections were formed. But in addition to the method, these also took over the errors of previous collections. The most distinguished of these are the *collectio regia*, which grouped the councils up to 1640 in thirty-seven volumes (Royal Printers in Paris, 1644), the collections of Philippus Labbaeus (1607-1667), and Gabriel Cossartius (1615-1674), Jesuits, with the councils up to 1664 in seventeen parts and eighteen volumes (Paris, 1671-1672). The last edition contains a quarter more conciliar prescriptions than the former. A part was added to it by Stephanus Baluzius (1630-1718) in Paris in 1683. The French clergy called upon Joannes Harduinus (1646-1729) to compile the *Collectio Regia Maxima* in eleven parts and twelve volumes (Royal Printers in Paris, 1714-1715). This Jesuit dedicated it to Louis XIV. Because it attacked Gallicanism, primarily in parts one and nine, it was condemned in 1716 by the French Parliament. It could not be sold, and the complete edition was destroyed. It was published in 1725 after a "correction." It is of such great importance that it is still regularly consulted. Indeed, it contains material from the councils up to 1714 and from many other sources that cannot be found in previous collections. It eliminated useless and obsolete notes and reviewed the manu-

scripts. It has five indexes: of the popes, of the councils, of the bishops and other conciliar participants, of the principal facts and words, and of the geographical division of the dioceses.

Less impressive is the collection of Nicolaus Coleti (1680-1765) in twenty-three parts, which covers the councils up to 1726 (Venice, 1728-1733).

209. The work of Joannes Dominicus Mansi, a priest of the Congregation of the Regular Clergy of the Mother of God and later Archbishop of Lucca, was ambitiously conceived. It contained material from the councils up to 1439 (Council of Florence) and was published in thirty-one volumes (1759-1798): the first thirteen of these in Florence, the following eighteen (since 1769) in Venice. It had no index. The collection was intended to be a standard for future editions and therefore it was called the *Sacrorum Conciliorum nova et amplissima collectio*.

Its size, however, was no guarantee of its quality. It is incomplete, uncritical, poorly arranged, and unreliable. The revisions of Joannes Baptista Martin, a priest and professor at the Catholic University of Lyons († 1922) and of Ludovicus Petit, an Assumptionist and archbishop of Athens († 1927), which were more carefully conceived, could not improve the quality of Mansi's work. These men published an anastatic reprint in 1901 (*reimpressio sine correctione "promissa,"* cf. A. Stickler, *op. cit.*, p. 298). They composed an introduction in a part "O" and compiled the *Capitularia regum Francorum* of Stephanus Baluzius into volumes 17bis and 18bis. They added the recent acts of the councils up to 1727, largely copied out of the collection of Nicolaus Coleti. They produced a work of thirty-five volumes, which was published in Paris and Leipzig in 1901-1904.

210. Much more reliable is the continuation of the collection of Mansi by Martin-Petit under the title *Collectio conciliorum recentiorum Ecclesiae Universae*. It brings into one part of three volumes supplements to the thirty-five parts up to 1720, and contains an alphabetic index of the councils. The last seventeen parts of the fifty-three volumes contain prescriptions of the

Eastern councils up to 1902 and the Western up to Vatican I (1870). This collection was completed in 1927 and is the last general collection. In 1960-1962, an anastatic reprint was published in Graz (53 vols). A modern edition is the Microcard Edition of Washington, 1961.

In spite of the gigantic work of Martin-Petit, there is still no complete and satisfactory edition of the conciliar documents. The *collectiones* offer a beginning but they must still be supplemented and improved by later private collections.

For an exemplary list of collections which cover specific regions or eras and have their own individual character, we refer to A. Stickler, *op. cit.*, pp. 285-294 and J. Gaudemet, *op. cit.*, pp. 40-44. For specific, period-related collections, we refer to:

H.T. BRUNS, *Canones Apostolorum et Conciliorum veterum saeculorum IV-VII*, 2 vols. Berlin, 1839 (anastatic reprint, Turin, 1958).
G. SCHNEEMANN (1829-1885) - T. GRANDERATH (1839-1902) (eds.), *Acta et decreta conciliorum recentiorum. Collectio Lacensis*, 7 vols., Freiburg im Breisgau, 1870-1890. — This is the complete edition by the Jesuits of Maria Laach of the *collectio Harduini* and covers 1682-1870.
C.H. TURNER (ed.), *Ecclesiae occidentalis monumenta iuris antiquissima*, 2 vols., Oxford, 1899-1939.
E. SCHWARTZ (ed.,) *Acta Conciliorum œcumenicorum (a concilio Ephesino a. 431 ad conc. Constantinopolitanum a. 879)*, Strassburg-Berlin-Leipzig, 1914, and continuation by J. STRAUB.

## Works on Papal and Conciliar Acts:

F. CLAEYS-BOUUAERT, "Bullaire," *Dictionnaire de droit canonique, vol. II, 1937, col. 1121-1126.*
N. JUNG, "Concile," *Dictionnaire de droit canonique*, vol. III, 1941, col. 1268-1301.
G. MOLLAT, "Lettres pontificales," *Dictionnaire de droit canonique*, vol. VI, 1955, col. 408-416.
C. HEFELÈ-H. LECLERCQ, *Histoire des conciles d'après les documents originaux*, 18 vols., Paris, 1907-1952.
G. DUMEIGE (ed.), *Histoire des conciles œcuméniques*, 12 vols., Paris, 1962-1981.
P. PALAZZINI, *Dizionario dei Concili*, 6 vols., Rome, 1963-1968.
*Annuarium Historiae Conciliorum. Internationale Zeitschrift für Konziliengeschichtsforschung*, Amsterdam, 1969-1970, Paderborn, 1971-.
H. JEDIN, *Kleine Konziliengeschichte. Die zwanzig Ökumenischen Konzilien im Rahmen der Kirchengeschichte*, Freiburg-Basel-Vienna, 1979[10].

*Konziliengeschichte*, new edition by W. BRANDMÜLLER, Paderborn, 1979 — (Reihe A: *Darstellungen*; Reihe B: *Untersuchungen*).

J. SAWICKI, *Bibliographia synodorum particularium*, (*Monumenta iuris canonici*, ser. C: *subsidia*, vol. 2), Città del Vaticano, 1967, and supplements in *Traditio* 24 (1968), pp. 508-511, 26 (1970), pp. 470-479; *Bulletin of Medieval Canon Law* 1 (1971), pp. 57-61, 2 (1972), pp. 91-139, 4 (1974), pp. 87-92, 6 (1976), pp. 95-100.

3) Collections of the Acts of the Roman Curia

212. The various congregations, tribunals, and offices of the Roman Curia have their own collections. They are very voluminous and often include unpublished collections. We refer for this to A. Stickler, *op. cit.*, pp. 318-362.

213. Bibliography (A 1-3)

A. VAN HOVE, *o.c.*, nos. 392-399.
A. STICKLER, *o.c.*, pp. 285-362.
P. ANDRIEU-GUITRANCOURT, *o.c.*, pp. 578-597, 815-846.
W.M. PLÖCHL, *o.c.*, vol. V, pp. 273-301.

B) Liturgical Books

214. There had been prayer books and song books in which the liturgy was regulated (cf. above, no. 72). The Council of Trent, however, did not issue regulations for the liturgy, since the popes were charged with its reform. The popes promulgated for the universal church the *Breviarium Romanum* in 1568, the *Missale Romanum* in 1570, the *Martyrologium* in 1584, the *pontificale Romanum* in 1596, the *Caeremoniale Episcoporum* in 1600, the *Rituale Romanum* in 1614, the *Memoriale Rituum* in 1725, and the *Libri Cantus* starting in 1905.

Most of these liturgical books were often subject to ratifications and revisions.

C) Attempts to Compose New Codifications

215. In the former periods, all energy was devoted to the editing and publication of law-collections (officially promulgated

or not). There was no thought of compiling a practical textbook for use in law-schools. The Perugian professor Joannes Paulus Lacelotti (1522-1590) tried to fill this gap with his *Institutiones iuris canonici*. Following the method of Justianian's *Institutiones*, it consisted of three parts (*personae, res, actiones*) and four books (*de personis, de rebus, de iudiciis, de criminibus et paenis*).

Pope Paul IV (1555-1559) gave official permission for the work in 1557 but later refused to promulgate it. When his successor Pius IV (1559-1565) also refused promulgation, Lancelotti published his work privately in Perugia in 1563 under the title of *Institutiones iuris canonici, quibus ius pontificium singulari methodo libris quattuor comprehenditur* and dedicated it to Pius IV.

As a private textbook, however, it had considerable authority. It was used and commented on in law-schools and many editions of the *Corpus Iuris Canonici* reproduced it as a supplement. In 1605, Pope Paul V allowed it to be printed as part of the *Corpus*.

The work witnesses to the quality of law-schools in the sixteenth century. In view of its juridical accuracy, clear formulation, and convenient structuring, it can be considered as a conclusion to the *Corpus Iuris Canonici*, and perhaps as its zenith. It is thus not surprising that the *Codex Iuris Canonici* of 1917 adopted a great deal of it.

216. Petrus Mattheus, a canonist in Lyons (1563-1621), tried in 1590 to give an official character to his work, the *Liber septimus Decretalium*, which he set up following the order of the *Liber Sextus*. The collection contains, apart from a few earlier ones, most decretals from Sixtus IV (1471-1484) to Sixtus V (1585-1590) and the canons of the Councils of Constance, Florence, and Lateran V. Even though it was added immediately to an edition of the *Corpus*, it never acquired official status. On the contrary, it was placed on the Index in 1623, and was not removed until 1911.

217. With the Council of Trent (1545-1563), a new view on law developed. The popes discovered that there was no systematic order in the disciplinary conciliar decretals and that there was a lack of harmony between the old and the new rules of law. In

order to give the conciliar prescriptions a place in the law, Gregory XIII established about 1580 a commission of three cardinals to prepare a new collection, an aggiornamento. It was intended to supplement and improve the *Corpus Iuris Canonici*.

Only under his successor, Clement VIII, who had been a member of this commission, were a few copies of the *Clementis VIII Decretales* printed in Rome in 1598. They contained canons of the Councils of Florence and Lateran I, and decretals of Trent, as well as papal acts from Gregory IX (1227) to Clement VIII (1605), which were not included in the *Corpus Iuris Canonici*. Therefore, its compiler called it the *Liber septimus Decretalium Clementis VIII*. The subjects were ordered in the traditional way, in books, titles, and chapters. However, neither Clement VIII nor his successors ratified the collection.

The custom of appending new law-books to the earlier corpus went out of practice; many of the earlier norms could no longer be applied in the new circumstances. The short and impersonal rules of conduct employed by the French kings were more appealing.

218. Benedict XIV (1740-1758) undertook one last attempt to supplement the *Corpus Iuris Canonici* with authentic collections through the four volumes of his *Bullarium*. He officially promulgated only the first volume by means of the constitution *Iam fere sextus* of 1746, which he sent to the university of Bologna. It consists of 146 constitutions that he himself had promulgated up to 4 January 1746. The other three volumes maintained their private character.

219. Bibliography

A. Van Hove, *o.c.*, no. 390.
A. Stickler, *o.c.*, pp. 308, 362-366.
P. Andrieu-Guitrancourt, *o.c.*, pp. 780-785.
W. Plöchl, *o.c.*, vol. V, pp. 267-273.
C. Lefèbvre, "Le premier volume du Bullaire de Benoît XIV constitue-t-il une collection authentique?," *L'Année canonique*, vol. XVII: *Mélanges offerts à Pierre Andrieu-Guitrancourt*, Paris, 1973, pp. 615-621.

CECCHELLI, M. (ed.), *Benedetto XIV (Prospero Lambertini). Convegno Internazionale di studi storici, Cento, 6-9 dicembre 1979* (centro Studi «Girolamo Baruffialdi». Documenti e studi, 3), 2 vols., Cento, 1981-1982.

## Chapter III

# THE SCIENCE OF LAW AND ITS PRACTITIONERS

A) To 1800

220. Up to the end of the seventeenth century, the science of law was practiced according to the ancient exegetical and arbitrary method. The ancient exegetical method had always been used in the schools. It treated all the chapters in the order in which they appeared in the books and in the titles of the decretals. The arbitrary method treated the special topics of canon law, spread out over several chapters in the decretals, in a systematic way.

Around 1670, Enricus Pirhing (1606-1679), professor at Dillingen, combined the two methods. His *methodus Pirhingana* treated all the chapters in the titles of the decretals systematically. The same approach had already been used in the textbooks of authors such as Lancelotti and Cucchus and in the *summae*, but these did not present a complete overview of canon law.

221. The jurists of the seventeenth and eighteenth century studied the *Decretum Gratiani*, the *Decretales Gregorii IX*, and the *Clementinae*, and developed their considerations and comments in confrontation with the decrees of the Council of Trent, the constitutions of the popes, and the practice of the Roman Curia, and treated these, as it was called: *in unico contextu*.

222. In the beginning of the seventeenth century, the jurists created new forms for their writings. In the *Introductiones*, the history of the sources and of the science of canon law were briefly described, together with general principles of the science of law: *praecognoscenda ad studium iuris canonici*.

Joannes Douiatius (Doujat) (1609-1688), a professor in Paris, published his *Praenotionum canonicarum libri quinque* in 1687.

Similar compositions such as the *Praecognita iuris canonici* (Ingolstadt, 1749) by Franciscus Xaverius Zech (1692-1772), a Jesuit and professor in Ingolstadt, the *Institutionum iuris ecclesiastici* (Augsburg, 1791) by Jacobus Antonius zum Thurn von Zallinger (1735-1813), a Jesuit and professor in Ausgburg, and the *Introductio ad ius ecclesiasticum catholicorum* (Vienna, 1774) by Joannes Valentinus Eybel (1741-1805), a professor in Vienna, were primarily directed against Protestantism.

The first commentators of this period still used the exegetical method: Henricus Wangnereck (1595-1664), a Jesuit and professor at Dillingen, in his *Commentarius exegeticus sacrorum canonum* (Dillingen, 1672), and Augustinus Barbosa (1590-1649) in his *Iuris ecclesiastici universi libri tres* (Lyons, 1634) and *Collectanea doctorum ... in ius pontificium universum* (Lyons, 1645) bear witness to a well-read and clear understanding and a fundamental approach. The *Ius canonicum seu commentaria absolutissima in quinque libros Decretalium* (Rome, 1661) of Prosper Fagnanus (1588-1678), secretary of the Congregation of the Council, is undoubtedly one of the most valuable works of this period. It gives a summary of medieval canonical writings. Paulus Layman (1574-1635), a Jesuit and professor at Ingolstatd, and Emanuel Gonzalez Tellez (+ ca. 1673), professor at Salamanca, are noteworthy jurists in this respect, too.

223. Enricus Pirhing used his new method is his book *Universum ius canonicum secundum titulos Decretalium distributum nova methodo explicatum* (Dillingen, 1674-1678). This work introduced the *Epocha Aurea*. His contemporaries, Ludovicus Engel (1634-1674), a Benedictine and professor at Salzburg, and Jacobus Wiestner (1640-1709), a Jesuit and professor at Ingolstadt, were the first to apply the *methodus Pirhingana* in their tracts.

The *Ius canonicum universum* (Freising, 1700-1714) of Anacletus Reiffenstuel (1641/1642-1703), a Capuchin and professor at Freising, reflects a thorough knowledge of Roman law, of the commentaries of the classic period, and of modern canon law. The tenets are clearly presented in correct subdivisions and are summarized and annotated. This work was highly respected by all jurists.

Zegerus Bernardus Van Espen (1646-1728), who became a professor in Louvain in 1674, published a *Ius ecclesiasticum universum* (Louvain, 1700). This is a systematic tract that abandoned the traditional structure — the presentation of the subject matter according to the order of the decretals. Van Espen's book was condemned in 1704 by a decree of the Holy Office for its jansenistic and gallicanistic tendencies, and it was listed in the *Index*. Van Espen confirmed the authority of the royal courts to settle disputes concerning the scope of ecclesiastical immunity. This trend was also present in his later works, particularly in his *Tractatus de recursu ad principem* of 1725, in which he placed the jurisdiction of the secular court above that of the Church. It was, however, his position in the *responsio epistolaris* (1724), where he stated that the archbishop of Utrecht, appointed by the chapter without the consent of Rome, was validly and licitly consecrated that led to his condemnation by the university court on 7 February 1728. Van Espen appealed to the court and obtained a reprieve but not the *suspensio a divinis*. The process, however, never resulted in a judgment because, at the age of eighty, Van Espen went voluntarily into exile. He withdrew to the United Provinces, where he died on 2 October 1728. He was one of the great Louvain canonists[1].

Franciscus Schmalzgrueber (1663-1735), a Jesuit and professor at Ingolstadt and Dillingen, followed the structure of A. Reiffenstuel so that his *Ius Ecclesiasticum universum* (Ingolstadt, 1717) was the best adapted to the requirements of practice.

The *Epocha Aurea* was concluded by Franciscus Schmier (1680-1728), a Benedictine and professor at Salzburg, Vitus Pichler (1670-1736), a Jesuit and professor at Ingelstadt and Placidus Böckhn (1690-1752), a Benedictine and professor at Salzburg. The *Iuris canonici universi publici et privati libri V* (Rome, 1803-

---

[1] M. Nuttinck, *La vie et l'œuvre de Zeger-Bernard Van Espen. Un canoniste janséniste, gallican et régalien à l'université de Louvain (1646-1728)*, Louvain, 1969.

1815) of Joannes Devoti (1744-1820) is well known, although it only dealt with the first three books of the Decretals.

224. Many others did not use the *methodus Pirhingana*, although their works were no less respected for that. It is sufficient here to list them: Franciscus Zypaeus (Vanden Zype) of Mechelen (1580-1650), Joannes Honorius van Axel de Seny of Utrecht, whose work dates from 1628, Henricus Zoesius († 1627), and Valerius Andreas (1588-1655), both of whom were professors of Louvain. The *Synopsis iuris canonici* of Valerius Andreas proved to be very useful. Shorter commentaries in which only the subject matter of the various chapters was explained were called *paratitla* or *margarithae*, such as the *Paratitla iuris canonici summaria et methodica explicatio Decretalium Gregorii papae IX* (Louvain, 1628) of Andreas Vallensis (Del Vaulx) (1569-1636), professor at Louvain, which was reprinted several times in Louvain, Antwerp, Cologne, Lyons, and Geneva, and the *Paratitla in V libros Decretalium Gregorii IX* (Toulouse, 1645) of Innocentius Cironius († ca. 1650), professor at Toulouse.

Finally, Andreas Alciatus (1492-1550), Jacobus Cuiacius (Cujas) (1520-1590) (cf. above), and his student, Joannes a Costa (1560-1637) also wrote commentaries of the decretals.

The eighteenth century textbooks based on the method of J.P. Lancelotti and M.A. Cucchus were still very successful in the nineteenth century. They were used in seminaries and schools. The text of the *Institutionum canonicarum libri IV* (Rome, 1785) by Joannes Devoti, for instance, contained only the law of the time, but the footnotes provided useful historical background information.

225. Under the influence of Gallicanism, Josephism, and the *Schola iuris naturalis*, many writings containing dubious theories appeared around 1750, particularly in Austria, France, Germany, Italy, and the southern Low Countries. They dealt primarily with the attitude of the Protestants towards the *Corpus Iuris Canonici* and with the authority of the state in religious matters (*sacra*). The titles of these works often revealed the convictions of their

authors. So, for example, Iustus Henning Böhmer (1655-1728), a professor at Halle, published the *Ius ecclesiasticum protestantium* (Halle, 1714-1737).

226. In this period, scholars discovered the value of indexes (*repertorium*) and scientific dictionaries (*lexicon iuris*), although they existed already in the Middle Ages. The *Repertorium iuris civilis et canonici* (Lyons, 1675) of Augustinus Barbosa and particularly the *Prompta bibliotheca canonica, iuridica, moralis, theologica, necnon ascetica, polemica, rubricistica, historica* (Bologna, 1746) of Lucius Ferraris († 1763), a Franciscan, met with widespread approval. The great utility of repertoria is proven by the numerous reprints of and supplements to Ferraris's work.

The dictionaries of Joannes Calvinus (Kahl) (°ca. 1570), a professor at Heidelberg, and of Augustinus Barbosa and the *Glossarium ad scriptores mediae et infimae latinitatis* (Paris, 1678) of Carolus Dufresne Du Cange (1610-1688), which was frequently republished and revised, have clearly demonstrated their reliability. They are still consulted today.

A few writers limited themselves to special subjects and produced very detailed and well developed tracts. Petrus Rebuffus (1487-1557), a professor in Paris, dealt with benefices (*Praxis beneficiorum*, Venice, 1554-1560) and concordats (*Tractatus concordatorum*, Paris, 1538). Martinus ab Azpilcueta or Navarrus (1492-1586), a professor at Salamanca and Coimbra in Portugal from 1538 to 1555, treated various subjects in his *Consilia et responsa* (Lyons, 1594). Didacus de Covarrubias a Leyva (1512-1577), a professor at Salamanca, in his *Epitome de sponsalibus et matrimoniis* (1545), and Thomas Sanchez (1551-1610), a Jesuit, in his *De sancto matrimonii sacramento* (Genoa, 1602), dealt with marriage.

The outstanding canonist, Prosper Lambertini, published in Bologna, in 1731, the *Institutiones ecclesiasticae* and in 1734-1738 *De Servorum Dei beatificatione et beatorum canonizatione*, (4 vols.). During his pontificate, Benedictus XIV (1740-1758) published, in 1748, *De synodo dioecesana*, with an immediate reprint in 1755.

The *Consilia* and *Consultationes* of Joannes Wamesius (1524-1590), professor at Louvain, of Franciscus Zypaeus, Jacobus Pignatelli (eighteenth century), Franciscus Schmalzgrueber and Franciscus Schmier also belong in this category.

227. Finally, we have to mention historical works. These treat the history of the sources, of the science of canon law, and of the ecclesiastical institutions in great detail. Next to the Spaniard Antonius Augustinus (1517-1586), Archbishop of Tarragone in 1576, who can be called the father of the critical study of the sources of the law, we find Ludovicus Thomassinus (1619-1695), an Oratorian, who studied the canonical institutions in an ingenious way. His magistral work *Ancienne et nouvelle discipline de l'Eglise touchant les bénéfices et les bénéficiers* (Paris, 1678-1679; 3 vols., 1679-1681), shows his knowledge of the origin and the development of ecclesiastical institutions. Pope Innocent XI requested a Latin translation of this work. This was done by Thomassinus himself and published in 1688 in Paris in three volumes under the title *Vetus et nova Ecclesiae disciplina circa beneficia et beneficiarios*. In the form of an alphabetical and updated dictionary by J.J. Bourassé (1813-1870), it was published in Paris in 1856 in French, in two volumes, and was included in J.P. Migne's *Encyclopédie théologique*. Joannes Franciscus André (1809-1880) reorganized the French edition according to the Latin principles, not chronologically but systematically, and then corrected it and added more material.

228. In commentaries on moral theology, one could commonly find specific observations on canon law. Some of them are still quite useful to the study of canon law, for instance the *Tractatus de legibus et Deo legislatore* (1612) from the *Opera Omnia* of Franciscus Suarez (Granada, 1548-1617). In spite of the fact that its major concern is not canon law, laws are dealt with as regards origin, nature, publication, and enforceability in such a way that this work on moral theology still influences writings on civil and canon law.

From the endless list of moralists, the most eminent are the Spanish Jesuits Ludovicus Molina († 1600), Joannes Azor († 1603), Gabriël Vasquez († 1604), Joannes de Salas († 1612), Fernandus de Castro Palao († 1633), and Joannes de Lugo († 1660). Authors from the Southern Law Countries include Leonardus Lessius († 1623), a Jesuit, Franciscus Silvius (Du Bois) († 1649), professor at Douai, and the Franciscan Guillielmus Herincx († 1678) from Holland. Among the works of Saint Alphonse of Liguori (Naples, 1696-1787), who founded the Redemptorists in 1732, the *Theologia moralis* is of particular importance for canon law.

The canonical jurists Paulus Laymann and Anacletus Reiffenstuel published their *Theologia moralis* in 1625 and 1692 respectively.

### 229. Bibliography

A. Van Hove, *o.c.*, nos. 494-523.
B. Kurtscheid-F. Wilches, *o.c.*, pp. 278-301.
W. Plöchl, *o.c.*, vol. V, pp. 348-362.
P. Andrieu-Guitrancourt, *o.c.*, pp. 1307-1318.
L. Müller, *Kirche, Staat, Kirchenrecht. Der Ingolstädter Kanonist Franz Xavier Zech (1692-1772)*, Regensburg, 1986 (Eichstätter Studien, Neue Folge, vol. XXII).

### 230. General Bibliography of the Third Period

C. Lefèbvre-M. Pacaut-L. Chevalier, *L'époque moderne (1563-1789), Les sources du droit et la seconde centralisation romaine* (*Histoire du droit et des institutions de l'Église en Occident*, vol. XV), Paris, 1976.

### B) From 1800 to the *Codex Iuris Canonici* (1917)

231. The first half of the nineteenth century (1800-1860) was characterized primarily by the waning influence and even decline of canon law. Canon law presented itself as a closed system. The ecclesiastical legislator was not sufficiently flexible to adapt the rigid rules to the changed circumstances of time and place. Thus,

in the mission countries, the bishops themselves legislated and arbitrarily disregarded the *ius canonicum universale*. In the universal Church, useless and obsolete prescriptions remained and often contradicted new laws. This led to great controversies about the validity of the old as well as the new regulations. The study of canon law became practically impossible. Thus, the French bishops could say in 1869:

> «Obruimur legibus. Hinc fit ut studium iuris canonici infinitis prope et inextricabilibus difficultatibus implicetur, controversiis ac processibus latissimis locus pateat, et conscientiae mille anxietatibus angantur et in contemptum legum impellantur.»
> Cf. P. Gasparri, *Codex Iuris Canonici 1917, praefatio*.

232. However, canon law had much to endure from exterior forces as well. The reformers of French society were anything but church-minded. They interfered in the appointment of bishops, in episcopal policy, in the training of priests, in the administration of parishes, and even in the internal organization of monasteries, many of which were suppressed or secularized. The new political concepts were in opposition to the political power of the Pope. The idea of direct participation in government (all power resides in the people) and rising materialism constituted a challenge to papal primacy in both religious and secular matters.

Gradually, however, the Pope succeeded in consolidating his authority, and scholars again defended the "true doctrine" and commented on papal decisions. From 1860 to the publication of the 1917 Code, the situation improved for the study of canon law.

233. The situation for the teaching of canon law was not much better in that period. Canon law was treated in the course of moral theology. Hardly any attention was given to the history of canon law. In seminaries, study houses of religious orders and congregations, and even at the universities, there was no demand for canon law. Not only the parochial clergy, but also the members of the episcopal curias knew little or nothing of canon law.

To correct this situation, a faculty of canon law was established at the Gregorian University in Rome in 1876 after a similar institute had been founded in the papal atheneum of the Lateran in 1853. This example was followed by the Anselmum in 1888 and by the Angelicum in 1896. The Louvain faculty of canon law was given new life with the reestablishment of the university in 1834. The Catholic University of Washington established a school of canon law in 1898.

234. Writings about canon law were scarce up to about 1860. There is only sporadic mention of studies on the history of the sources, such as that by Augustinus Theiner (1804-1875), an Oratorian and later Prefect of the Vatican archives, who published his *Disquisitiones criticae in praecipuas canonum et decretalium collectiones seu sylloges Gallandianae continuatio* in Rome in 1836. The commentators on canon law hardly breached the threshold of anonimity.

After 1860, the increasing influence of canon law was reflected in the scientific literature. In 1870, Fredericus Maasen (1823-1900) published a very valuable *Geschichte der Quellen und der Literatur des canonischen Rechts im Abendlande*. Joannes Fredericus von Schulte (1827-1914), professor at Prague and later at Bonn, and Adolphe Tardif (1823-1890), professor at the *Ecole des Chartes* in Paris, published their history of canon law in this period (cf. above, p. 25). The commentators on canon law increased greatly in number, and canon law as a field of study was rediscovered. Witnesses to this are:

J. FERRARI, *Summa institutionum canonicarum*, Genoa, 1847.
Ph. DE ANGELIS, *Praelectiones iuris canonici ad methodum decretalium Gregorii IX*, Rome, 1877-1891.
F.X. WERNZ, *Ius Decretalium*, 7 vols., Rome - Prato, 1905-1914.
G. PHILLIPS, *Kirchenrecht*, 7 vols., Regensburg, 1845-1872 (anastatic reprint, Graz, 1959).
J.F. von SCHULTE, *Lehrbuch des katholischen Kirchenrechts*, Giessen, 1863; rev. ed.: *Lehrbuch des katholischers und evangelischen Kirchenrechts*, 1886.
F.H. VERING, *Lehrbuch des katholischen und protestantischen Kirchenrechts*, Freiburg im Breisgau, 1874-1876, 1893[3].

D. CRAISSON, *Manuale totius iuris canonici*, Paris, 1861, 1899[9].
ID., *Elementa iuris canonici ad usum seminariorum*, Poitiers, 1866.
J.B. SÄGMULLER, *Lehrbuch des katholischen Kirchenrechts*, 2 vols., Freiburg im Breisgau, 1900-1902, 1925-1934[4].
D. PRÜMMER, *Manuale iuris ecclesiastici*, Freiburg im Breisgau, 1907-1909.
E. FRIEDBERG, *Lehrbuch des katholischen und evangelischen Kirchenrechts*, Leipzig, 1879, 1909[6].
S. AICHNER, *Compendium iuris ecclesiastici*, Brixen, 1862, 1915[12].
R. SCHERER, *Handbuch des Kirchenrechts*, 2 vols., Graz, 1886-1898.
H.J. FEYE, *De impedimentis et dispensationibus matrimonialibus*, Louvain, 1903.
P. DE BRABANDERE, *Iuris canonici et iuris canonico-civilis compendium*, Bruges, 1866-1869, 1903[8].
D. BOUIX, *Institutiones iuris canonici in varios tractatus divisae*, Paris, 1861-1869.
OWEN, *Institutes of Canon Law*, London, 1884.

In this same period, specific commentaries were made on public canon law:

J. SOGLIA, *Institutiones juris publici et privati ecclesiastici*, 2 vols in 1, 's Hertogenbosch, 1865[10].
C. TARQUINI, *Institutiones iuris publici ecclesiastici*, Rome, 1860, 1896[16]. Translation in French by A. ONCLAIR in 1868.
M. LIBERATORE, *La Chiesa e lo stato christiano, La Chiesa e lo stato christiano*, Napoli, 1871. *Del diritto pubblico ecclesiastico*, Prato, 1887; Translation in French by A. ONCLAIR in 1888.
F. MOULART, *L'Église et l'État ou les deux puissances. Leur origine, leurs relations, leurs droits et leurs limites*, (Louvain-Paris, 1895[4]. German translation: *Kirche und Staat oder die beiden Gewalten*, 1881, anastatic reprint, Aalen, 1974).
F. CAVAGNIS, *Institutiones iuris publici ecclesiastici*, 3 vols., Rome, 1882-1883, 1904[4].
F.M. CAPPELLO, *Institutiones iuris publici ecclesiastici*, Rome, 1907-1908 (Turin, 1913).

To aid teaching and to promote the science of law, encyclopedias, lexicons, and sources were published, along with important journals. Cf. A. Van Hove, *op. cit.*, nos. 529-553; B. Kurtscheid-F.A. Wilches, *op. cit.*, pp. 310-330.

FOURTH PERIOD
# THE *CODEX IURIS CANONICI* OF 1917, ITS COMMENTATORS, AND ITS REVISION IN 1983

CHAPTER I

HISTORICAL BACKGROUND AND PREPARATION

235. It gradually became clear that canon law urgently needed to be revised. Pope Pius IX, on 6 December 1864, asked the cardinals for their opinion, and they expressed themselves almost unanimously for the convening of a general council. In spite of the efforts of many bishops to have a *collectio canonum*, a code of canon law in which all the laws then in force would be included, the Council considered only purely dogmatic questions. When the Council was suspended, on 20 October 1870, because of the Franco-Prussian War, no advances had been made on the disciplinary level since 1864.

Nevertheless, the work of the council fathers was not in vain: the many *vota* and *schemata* that they had drafted formed an excellent preparation for the later codification that would be compiled by a college of cardinals under the direction of Pietro Gasparri in 1917.

236. Pius X dreamt of a codification of the law in force from the start of his pontificate in August 1903. To this end, he promulgated, on 19 March 1904, the Motu proprio *Arduum sane*, which established a *collegium consultorum* in addition to the *peculiare Cardinalium consilium*.

On 13 November 1904, the *collegium* met. In 1912, the advice of bishops and superiors general was requested regarding the first and the second books. Books three and five were submitted to them in 1913 and book four in 1914. In 1916, the improved draft was sent comprehensive codification of canon law in the constitution *Providentissima Mater Ecclesia*, which appears in the *Acta Apostolicae Sedis* of 28 June 1917. One year later, on May 19, 1918, it went into force as the universal, exclusive, but also relative — which means with the exclusion of all former contrary prescriptions, but including old rules on matters not included in this Code — law of the Church.

A Motu proprio of September 15, 1917, established a commission of cardinals to answer questions from bishops and superiors general. It was responsible for the authentic interpretation of this Code.

This codification had some predecessors, such as the *Ius Decretalium* of Franciscus-Xaverius Wernz, published in Rome (1889-1903); the *Ius canonicum generale distributum in articulos*, Paris, 1890, by Albert Pillet; the *Memento iuris publici et privati*, Paris, 1895, by Deshayes; the *Codex Sanctae Catholicae Romanae Ecclesiae*, Rome, 1898-1902, by Enrico Pezzani, and the *Iuris canonici privati codex vigens, sive legum ecclesiasticarum novissima collectio*, Palermo, 1904, by Fortunato Russo.

Chapter II

# THE *CODEX IURIS CANONICI* OF 1917

237. Pietro Gasparri (1852-1934) obviously played a very important role in the birth of the CIC of 1917. As professor of canon law at the *Institut Catholique de Paris*, he had already written a *Tractatus canonicus de ordinatione* (2 vols., 1883), a *Tractatus canonicus de SS. Eucharistia* (2 vols., 1897), and a *Tractatus canonicus de matrimonio* (2 vols., $1932^4$).

On 2 January 1898, he was appointed secretary of the Congregation for Extraordinary Matters and in 1904 secretary of the Commission of Cardinals for the Code. His objective was not only to make a codification of existing law but also to establish a collection of all the sources that were used for it. He published the first six volumes of the *Codicis iuris canonici fontes* (Rome, 9 vols., 1923-1939), and Iustinianus Serédi (1884-1945) published the last three.

He included all the texts *ex toto vel ex parte* of councils, popes, and congregations, insofar as the Code referred to them, with the exception of the texts of the *Corpus Iuris Canonici* and of the Council of Trent, since he assumed that everybody already had these. This private work is invaluable to canonists for the interpretation of the texts in the light of their history and origin.

As the Secretary of State, Gasparri signed the Lateran treaty on 11 February 1929 with Mussolini. He died in Rome on November 18, 1934.

Eugenio Pacelli, the later Pope Pius XII, was the secretary of the commission and, in this capacity, made a major contribution to the editorial work of the Code.

238. Bibliography

F. CIMETIER, *Les sources du droit ecclésiastique*, Paris, 1930, pp. 150-197.
R. NAZ, "Codex iuris canonici," in *Dictionnaire de droit canonique*, vol. III, 1942, col. 909-940.

R. Naz, "Collections de droit canoniques," *Dictionnaire de droit canonique*, vol. III, 1942, col. 988-990.
B. Kurtscheid-F.A. Wilches, *o.c.*, pp. 340-349.
A. Stickler, *o.c.*, vol. V, pp. 301-308.
P. Andrieu-Guitrancourt, *o.c.*, pp. 879-896.
W.M. Plöchl, *o.c.*, vol. V, pp. 301-308.
A. Giacobbi, *o.c.*, pp. 313-329.
R. Epp, C. Lefèbvre, R. Metz, *Le droit et les institutions de l'Église catholique latine de la fin du XVIIIe siècle à 1978. Sources et Institutions* (Histoire du droit et des Institutions de l'Église en Occident, vol. XVI), Paris, 1981.
L. Chevaillier, C. Lefèbvre, R. Metz, *Le droit et les institutions de l'Église catholique latine de la fin du XVIIIe siècle à 1978. Organismes collégiaux et moyens de gouvernement* (Histoire du droit et des Institutions de l'Église en Occident, vol. XVII), Paris, 1982.
J.M. Aubert, R. Metz, G. Sicard, Ch. Wackenheim, P. Winninger, *Le droit et les institutions de l'Église catholique latine de la fin du XVIIIe siècle à 1978. Église et sociétés* (Histoire du droit et des Institutions de l'Église en Occident, vol. XVIII), Paris, 1984.
F.M. Taliani, *Vita del Cardinale Gasparri, segretario di Stato e povere prete*, Milan, 1938.
*La figura storica del Card. Pietro Gasparri di Ussita* (Università di Macerata, pubblicazioni della Facoltà di Giurisprudenza, nr. 15), Milan, 1977.

239. For the division of the Code, Gasparri abandoned the ancient content structure. Although he divided the collection into five books, in the fashion of the medieval official collections of decretals, he no longer ordered the canons under one of the five classic titles: *iudex, iudicium, clerus, sponsalia, crimen*. He divided his work according to the law books of the old Roman jurists, Gaius (I,8) and Justinianus (I,2,12) (*personae, res, actiones*) and the textbook of J.P. Lancelotti, the *Institutiones Iuris Canonici*, according to the proverb, *personas nos prima docet, resque secunda, tertia dat iudices, crimina quarta premit*. He added a general introduction, *normae generales*.

Each book is divided into *tituli*, each *titulus* into *capita* if necessary, and each *caput* into *articuli* if necessary. The Code has 2414 canons.

In the *normae generales* (86 canons), the law and customs are situated. The entire law concerning persons comprises 639 canons. By far the largest part is formed by the law with regard to *res* containing 826 canons that treat of, among other things, the sacraments, the *cultus divinus*, and the *magisterium ecclesiasticum*. The fourth book has 646 canons and describes procedure and procedural law concerning ordination. With its 220 canons, the fifth book, *de delictis et poenis*, is the smallest.

For a consideration of the mentality in which the Code was formed, we refer to U. Stutz, *Der Geist des Codex Iuris Canonici*, Stuttgart, 1918 (anastatic reprint, Amsterdam 1961); P. Shannon, "De Codex van het Kerkelijk Recht, 1918-1967," *Concilium*, 1967, pp. 49-57. P. LANDAU, "Ulrich Stutz und der Codex Iuris Canonici von 1917," *Zeitschrift der Savigny-Stiftung für Rechtsgeschichte. Kanonistische Abteilung* 74 (1988) 1-16.

240. The only authentic edition of the Code is in the *Acta Apostolicae Sedis* of June 28, 1917 (vol. IX, Part II). With the permission of the Holy See, new private editions appeared in which the official text was annotated with references to the sources and supplemented with a foreword by P. Gasparri, the Motu proprio of 15 September 1917, and an index.

241. Even though the CIC was so exhaustively planned and precisely worked out, it still could not escape the changing times. Amendments and supplements were regularly published in the *Acta Apostolicae Sedis*. Private collections compiled the interpretations of the Code, and new norms were issued to adapt it to the changed circumstances. C. Sartori-B. Belluco, *Enchiridion canonicum seu Sanctae Sedis responsiones post editum Codicem Iuris Canonici datae*, 11th edition (1917-1963), Rome, 1963, and E.F. Regatillo, *Interpretatio et iurisprudentia Codicis iuris canonici*, 3rd edition, Santander, 1953, compiled the answers of the papal commission regarding the interpretation of the Code. The pronouncements of the highest legal tribunal are found in the *S. Romanae Rotae decisiones seu sententiae*. X. Ochoa published a chronological account of all the prescriptions that were promul-

gated after the Code, even those which did not appear in the *AAS*, in his *Leges Ecclesiae post Codicem Iuris Canonici editae 1917-1978*, 5 vols., Rome, 1966-1980. Prior to Ochoa, S. Meyer, in his *Neueste Kirchenrechts-Sammlung (1917-1950)*, 4 vols., Freiburg im Breisgau, 1953-1962, had already made such an attempt, but according to the order of the canons. The Eastern Churches took a similar initiative in the *Codificazione canonica orientale. Fonti (Pontificia Commissio Codici iuris canonici orientalis recognoscendo: Fontes)*, Rome, 1930 -.

The 1917 Code, of course, superseded all the other collections. At last, the Catholic Church had its official, exclusive, and universal collection of laws. Obviously, commentaries would henceforth be made only on this collection.

242. From the long list of commentators, we cite only the most important and in chronological order.

C. BERUTTI, *Institutiones iuris canonici*, 6 vols., Turin, 1906-1943.
U. BESTE, *Introductio in Codicem*, Naples, 1961[5].
A. BLAT, *Commentarium textus Codicis iuris canonici*, 6 vols., Rome, 1921-1938[2].
L. BOUSCAREN-A.C. ELLIS, *Canon Law*, Milwaukee, 1963[4].
J. BRYS, *Iuris canonici compendium*, 2 vols., Bruges, 1947-1949[10].
A. CANCE, *Le code de droit canonique*, 4 vols., Paris, I-III, 1950-1952[8]; IV, 1949[2].
F.M. CAPPELLO, *Summa iuris canonici*, 3 vols., 1951-1955[4].
I. CHELODI-P. CIPROTTI, *Ius canonicum de matrimonio et de iudiciis matrimonialibus*, Vicenza, 1947[5].
I. CHELODI-P. CIPROTTI, *Ius canonicum de personis*, Vicenza, 1957[4].
H. CICOGNANI-D. STAFFA, *Commentatium ad librum I Codicis iuris canonici*, 2 vols., Rome, 1939-1941.
F. CLAEYS BOÚAERT-G. SIMENON, *Manuale iuris canonici*, 3 vols., Ghent-Liège, I, 1951[6]; II, 1947[3]; III, 1943[5].
M. CONTE A CORONATA, *Institutiones iuris ecclesiastici*, 5 vols., Turin, I-IV, 1950-1956[4]; V, 1951[3].
C. HOLBÖCK, *Handbuch des Kirchenrechts*, 2 vols., Innsbruck-Vienna, 1951.
E. JOMBART, *Manuel de droit canonique*, Paris, 1958[2].

H. JONE, *Gesetzbuch der lateinischen Kirche*, 3 vols., Paderborn, 1950-1953[2].

H. JONE, *Commentarium in Codicem Iuris Canonici*, 3 vols., Paderborn, 1950-1955[2].

M. LEGA, curante V. BARTOCCETTI, *Commentarius in iudicia ecclesiastica*, 3 vols., Rome (vol. I en II, 1950[2]; vol. II, 1941).

G. MICHIELS, *Normae generales iuris canonici*, 2 vols., Paris, 1949[2].
— *Principia generalia de personis in Ecclesia*, Paris, 1955[2].
— *De delictis et poenis*, 3 vols., Paris, 1961.
— *De potestate ordinaria et delegata*, Paris, 1964.

K. MÖRSDORF, *Die Rechtssprache des Codex Iuris Canonici*, Paderborn, 1937, (anastatic reprint 1967).
—, *Lehrbuch des Kirchenrechts auf Grund des Codex Iuris Canonici, begründet von Eduard Eichmann*, 3 vols., Munich-Paderborn-Vienna, 1964-1974[11].

G. OESTERLE, *Praelectiones iuris canonici* (liber I et II), Rome, 1931.

B. OJETTI, *Commentarium in Codicem iuris canonici*, 4 vols. Rome, 1927-1931.

E. REGATILLO, *Ius sacramentarium*, Santander, 1960[3].
— *Institutiones iuris canonici*, 2 vols., Santander, 1961[6].

A. RETZBACH, *Das Recht der katholischen Kirche*, Freiburg im Breisgau, 1953[4].

L. RODRIGO, *Tractatus de legibus*, Santander, 1944.

J. TORRE, *Processus matrimonialis*, Naples, 1956[3].

*Traité de droit canonique*, R. NAZ, 4 vols., Paris, 1955[2].

A. VAN HOVE, *De legibus ecclesiasticis*, Malines, 1930.
— *De consuetudine, de temporis supputatione*, Malines, 1933.
— *De rescriptis*, Malines, 1936.
— *De privilegiis, de dispensationibus*, Malines, 1939.

A. VERMEERSCH - J. CREUSEN, *Epitome iuris canonici*, 3 vols., Malines-Paris, I, 1963[8]; II, 1954[7]; III, 1956[7].

F.X. WERNZ - P. VIDAL, *Ius canonicum ad Codicis normam exactum*, 7 vols., Rome, I, 1952[2]; II, 1943[3]; III, 1933; IV, 1934-1936; V, 1946[3]; VI, 1949[2]; VII, 1951[2].

S. WOYWOD, *A Practical Commentary on the Code of Canon Law*, New York, 1952[2].

F. CAPPELLO, *Summa iuris publici ecclesiastici*, Rome, 1954[6].

A. OTTAVIANI, *Institutiones iuris publici ecclesiastici*, 2 vols., Rome, 1958-1960[4].

L.R. SOTILLO, *Compendium iuris publici ecclesiastici*, Santander, 1958[3].

G. Vromant, *Ius missionariorum*, 6 vols.:
— *Introductio et normae generales*, Bruges, 1959².
— *De personis*, Louvain, 1935².
— *De fidelium associationibus, de actione catholica, de legione Mariae*, Paris, 1955².
— *De matrimonio*, Paris, 1952³.
— *De bonis ecclesiae temporalibus*, Brussels, 1953³.
— *Facultates apostolicae*, Paris, 1947³.

CHAPTER III

# THE *CODEX IURIS CANONICI* OF 1983

243. In the 1950s, it was obvious that a thorough discussion on the Church, humankind, the world and their interrelationships was necessary. Canon law urgently needed revision, but this was not possible without a clear profile established by an ecumenical council. This intention Pope John XXIII made known on January 25, 1959. From 1962 to 1965, hundreds of Council Fathers discussed and examined the present problems of the Church and thus laid the basis for the new *Codex Iuris Canonici*. Their collaboration was essential so that the juridical formulation, which would apply for the universal Church, could be created as collegially as possible.

244. On March 28, 1963, Pope John XXIII established the *Pontificia Commissio Codici Iuris Canonici recognoscendo*. The chairman was Pietro Ciriaci and the secretary Mgr. Giacomo Violardo. But all forty members of the commission agreed that the revision of the Code itself should wait for the final accounts of the Council. On April 17, 1964, Pope Paul VI appointed seventy consultors and a permanent secretariat of seven members. They had to draw up the propositions for the new canons. Raymundus Bidagor became the new secretary, and Mgr. Willy Onclin was appointed as adjunct-secretary of the Commission. After the death of Cardinal Ciriaci, Mgr. Pericle Felici was appointed pro-president on February 21, 1967 and president on June 26. Mgr. Rosalio Castillo Lara became the new secretary on February 12, 1975 and followed Mgr. Pericle Felici as pro-president after his death on March 22, 1982. With all its later additions, the commission had some 180 members, both priests and laymen.

With the Solemn Session of November 20, 1965, in the presence of Paul VI, the work of the commission officially started.

The entire Code was reworked by various committees and rewritten canon by canon. In addition to the decisions of the Second Vatican Council, account was also taken of the principles that had been formulated by the first post-conciliar synod of bishops in 1967 in Rome. This preparatory phase extended from 1963 to 1972. The period of revision and reworking ran from 1973 to 1980.

A first draft was sent to all the bishops and universities for criticism in order to obtain the collegial collaboration of the universal Church. This closely followed the structure of the old Code. In 1980, a second draft, the *Schema Codicis Iuris Canonici recogniti*, was finished, and this completely differed both in structure and in spirit from the old Code. Published on the 29th of June 1980, it was presented to Pope John Paul II, who ordered the cardinals-members of the commission, together with seventy-four newly appointed members, to examine it critically. Their comments were sent to the consultors. In a final plenary session between 20 and 28 October 1981, the texts obtained a unanimous "placet." The final version was presented to the Pope on April 22, 1982. After a few last-minute changes, the *Codex Iuris Canonici* was promulgated on January 25, 1983 by the apostolic constitution *Sacrae Disciplinae Leges*. Precisely twenty-four years had elapsed since Pope John XXIII announced on January 25, 1959 that he wanted to review the Code. The official presentation took place on February 3 under the chairmanship of the Pope and in the presence of fifty-seven cardinals, the members of the Curia, the diplomatic corps accredited to the Holy See, the professors and the students of the papal faculties of canon law, and many jurists from various countries.

On November 27, 1983, the first Sunday of the new ecclesiastical year, the CIC of 1983 came into force. Cf. *AAS*, vol. LXXV, Part II, pp. VII-XIV; *Osservatore Romano* of 27 January 1983, *Archief van de Kerken*, vol. XXXVIII, pp. 25-28; *Communicationes* XV, I, 1983, pp. 3-8; *Appollinaris* LVI, 1983, pp. 5-11; *Documentation catholique* LXXX, 1983, pp. 244-247. The "errata" (102) appeared in *AAS*, vol. LXXV, Part II, pp. 321-

324. Although translated, only the Latin version has full authority.

Unlike the Code of 1917, the 1983 Code does not claim to be the only law-corpus, since several matters are not treated in it. These include the organization of the *Curia*, the election of the popes, beatification and canonization procedures and administrative jurisdiction.

245. Its 1752 canons are divided into seven books:

Book I     *De normis generalibus* (can. 1-203)
Book II    *De populo Dei* (can. 204-746)
Book III   *De Ecclesiae munere docendi* (can. 747-833)
Book IV   *De Ecclesiae munere sanctificandi* (can. 834-1253)
Book V    *De bonis Ecclesiae temporalibus* (can. 1254-1310)
Book VI   *De sanctionibus in Ecclesia* (can. 1311-1399)
Book VII *De processibus* (can. 1400-1752)

A detailed description of the genesis and the content can be found in the following works:

F. d'OSTILLO, *E'pronto il nuovo Codice di diritto canonico. Iter revisionale e prossima promulgazione*, Città del Vaticano, 1982.
B. FRANCK, *Vers un nouveau droit canonique*, Paris, 1983.
R. METZ, "La nouvelle codification du droit de l'Église (1959-1983)," *Revue de droit canonique* 33 (1983), pp. 110-168.
V. NUÑOZ ESTEBAN, "El nouvo Código de derecho canonico," *Studium. Revista quadrimestral de filosofia y teologia* 23 (1983), pp. 181-219.
P. TOCANEL, "Il nuovo Codice di diritto canonico," *Apollinaris* 56 (1983), pp. 70-88.
G. FRANSEN, "Le nouveau Code de droit canonique. Présentations et réflexions," *Revue théologique de Louvain* 14 (1983), pp. 275-288; ID., "Le nouveau Code de droit canonique," *Académie Royale de Belgique. Bulletin de la Classe des lettres et des Sciences morales et politiques*, series V, 69 (1983), pp. 321-335; ID., "New Code-New Perspectives," *The Jurist* 45 (1985), pp. 365-378.
J. PASSICOS, "La publication du Code de droit canonique pour l'Église latine. Un événement de l'Église en 1983," *Esprit et Vie. L'Ami du clergé* 93 (1983), pp. 42-47; ID., "Le nouveau Code de droit canonique. Expression du renouveau de l'Église," *Études* (1984), pp. 255-263.

J. HERRANZ, "Genesis del nuove Cuerpo legislativo de la Iglesia (de Código de 1917 al Código de 1983)," *Ius Canonicum* 23 (1983), pp. 491-526.

A. SCHEUERMANN, "Zur Einführung in den CIC 1983," in *Ordens-Korrespondenz* 24 (1983), pp. 391-403.

J. ABSIL, "Le nouveau Code de droit canonique. Sa visée spirituelle et pastorale," *La foi et le temps* 13 (1983), pp. 361-370.

G.V. LOBO, "New Code of Canon Law. — General Presentation," *Vidyajyoti. Journal of Theological Reflection* 47 (1983), pp. 158-178.

E. CAPPELLINI - M. MARCHESI, *Il nuovo Codice. Proposte di interpretazione e contenuto normativo*, Brescia, 1983, 154 p.

M. HUFTIER, "Le Code de droit canonique," *Esprit et Vie. L'Ami du clergé* 94 (1984), pp. 186-192, 218-219, 254-255, 286-287.

J. BEYER, "Le nouveau Code de droit canonique. Esprit et structures," *Nouvelle revue théologie* 106 (1984), pp. 360-382, 566-583. Cfr ID., "Il nuovo Codice di diritto canonico," *La scuola cattolica* 112 (1984), pp. 121-145.

W. ONCLIN, "Le nouveau Code de droit canonique," *Ephemerides theologicae Lovanienses* 60 (1984), pp. 325-345.

H.M. STAMM, "Die revision des Codex Iuris Canonici," *Antonianum* 59 (1984), pp. 52-70.

M. BONNET - B. DAVID, *Introduction au droit ecclésial et au nouveau Code* (les cahiers du droit ecclésial), Luçon, 1985, pp. 33-60 (chap. II: *Historique de la réforme du Code*).

J.B. BEYER, *Dal Concilio al Codice. Il nuovo Codice e le istanze del Concilio Vaticano II*, Bologna, 1984; ID., *Du concile au Code de droit canonique. La mise en application de Vatican II*, Paris, 1985.

S.A. EVART, "A Canonical Analysis of Essential Elements in Light of the 1983 Code of Canon Law," *The Jurist* 45 (1985), pp. 438-501.

Ecumenical Reflections on the Codex 1983.

J.O. DUKE, "The Code of Cann Law. A Protestant Perspective," *The Jurist* 46 (1986), pp. 347-375.

P. L'HUILLIER, "An Eastern Orthodox Viewpoint on the New Code of Canon Law," *The Jurist* 46 (1986), pp. 376-393. ID., "Le Code de droit canonique de 1983. Point de vue d'un orthodoxe," *L'Année canonique* 30 (1987), pp. 423-430.

J.R. WRIGHT, "The 1983 Code of Canon Law: An Anglican Evaluation," *The Jurist* 46 (1986), pp. 394-418.

246. A *Motu proprio* of 2 January 1984 created the *Pontificia Commissio Codici Iuris authentice interpretando* in order to provide authentic interpretations of, and additions to the new code of canon law.

The first translations that have appeared since 1983 are

*The Code of Canon Law in English Translation*, London, 1983.
*Code of Canon Law, Latin-English Edition*, Washington, 1983.
*Codex des kanonischen Rechtes. Lateinisch-deutsche Ausgabe*, Kevelaer, 1983.
*Codice di diritto canonico. Testo ufficiale e versione italiana*, Rome, 1984².
*Wetboek van canoniek recht. Latijns-Nederlandse Uitgave*, Brussels-Hilversum, 1987.

Translation with Commentary

*Código de Derecho Canónico* (Universidad de Navarra. Instituto Martin de Azpilcueta), Pamplona, 1983.
*Código de Derecho Canónico* (Facultad de derecho canónico de la Universidad Pontificia de Salamanca), Madrid, 1986⁷.
*The Code of Canon Law. A Text and Commentary* (The Canon Law Society of America), New York - Mahwah, 1985.
*Commento al Codice di diritto canonico*, Città del Vaticano, 1985.

Insofar as they already belong to history, we give a few commentaries on the new Code.

H. SCHWENDENWEIN, *Das neue Kirchenrecht. Gesamtdarstellung*, Graz-Vienna-Cologne, 1983.
J. LISTL-H. MÜLLER-H. SCHMITZ, *Handbuch des katholischen Kirchenrechts*, Regensburg, 1983.
N. RUF, *Das Recht der katholischen Kirche nach dem neuen Codex Iuris Canonici für die Praxis erläutert*, Freiburg-Basel-Vienna, 1983.
*La nuova legislazione canonica*, Rome, 1983, (*Studia Urbaniana*, 19).
*Il nuovo Codice di diritto canonico. Novitá, motivazione e significato*. Atti della settimano di studio 26-30 aprile 1983, Rome, 1983 (Utrumque Ius, 9).
E. CAPPELLINI (ed.), *La normativa del nuovo Codice*, Brescia, 1983.
K. WALF, *Einführung in das neue katholische Kirchenrecht*, Zurich-Einsiedln-Cologne, 1984.
R. PARALIEU, *Guide pratique du Code de Droit Canonique. Notes pastorales*, Bourges, 1985.

*Münsterischer Kommentar zum Codex Iuris Canonici*, Essen, 1985.
M. PETRONCELLI, *Diritto canonico*, Naples, 1985[9].
*Il nuovo Codice di diritto canonico. Studi,* Torino, 1985, *La Scuola Cattolica*, 112 (1984), pp. 119-393.

## Reference Books

K. OCHOA, *Index verborum ac locutionum Codicis iuris canonici*, Città del Vaticano 1984[2].

L. CHIAPETTA, *Dizionario del nuovo Codice di diritto canonico. Prontuario teorico – pratico*, Naples, 1986[2].